IERI Monograph Series

Issues and Methodologies in Large-Scale Assessments

SPECIAL ISSUE 1

**Sample Size Requirements in HLM:
An Empirical Study**

IERI

IEA ETS

October 2012

Foreword

For more than four years, members of the International Association for the Evaluation of Educational Achievement (IEA) and Educational Testing Service (ETS) have worked together within the IEA-ETS Research Institute (or IERI) on projects designed to improve the science of large-scale assessments of educational achievement. IERI undertakes activities focused on three broad areas of work: research studies related to the development and implementation of large-scale assessments, professional development and training, and dissemination of research findings and information gathered through large-scale assessments.

To date, IERI has published four volumes of the periodical *Issues and Methodologies in Large-Scale Assessments*. These volumes usually contain six to seven peer-reviewed papers. This publication is the first special issue. It is special because it contains only one (extended) paper. The paper's authors address a matter concerning hierarchical linear models (HLMs) that is highly relevant for researchers engaged in planning international large-scale studies, namely the relationship between the sample sizes at each level of a hierarchical model and the precision of the outcome model. Increasing or reducing the number of units of observation has significant implications for the costs of large-scale assessment studies. Consequently, it is of utmost importance to have the best figures possible at hand when planning large-scale assessment studies that produce data subject to later analysis via HLM and other multilevel approaches.

Given that HLM is such a popular method of analyzing large-scale assessment data, many researchers already consider the requirements for HLM analysis in their study designs. While several rules of thumb on the number of observations necessary at each level of analysis exist, an in-depth study addressing the sample-size requirements of the type presented in this paper has not previously been available.

We hope you will find reading this paper as interesting as we did. We also hope you will consider supporting this periodical by submitting papers presenting your own methodological research on international large-scale assessments to IERI. Finally, we would like to express our gratitude for the generous support given to this report by the National Center for Education Statistics in the United States.

Matthias von Davier and Dirk Hastedt
Editors of the IERI periodical *Issues and Methodologies in Large-Scale Assessments*

ABOUT IEA

The International Association for the Evaluation of Educational Achievement (IEA) is an independent, non-profit, international cooperative of national research institutions and governmental research agencies. Through its comparative research and assessment projects, IEA aims to:

- Provide international benchmarks that may assist policy-makers in identifying the comparative strengths and weaknesses of their education systems

- Provide high-quality data that will increase policy-makers' understanding of key school- and non-school-based factors that influence teaching and learning

- Provide high-quality data that will serve as a resource for identifying areas of concern and action, and for preparing and evaluating educational reforms

- Develop and improve the capacity of educational systems to engage in national strategies for educational monitoring and improvement

- Contribute to development of the worldwide community of researchers in educational evaluation.

Additional information about the IEA is available at www.iea.nl and www.iea-dpc. de.

ABOUT ETS

Educational Testing Service (ETS) is a non-profit institution whose mission is to advance quality and equity in education by providing fair and valid assessments, research, and related services for all people worldwide. In serving individuals, educational institutions

and government agencies around the world, ETS customizes solutions to meet the need for teacher professional development products and services, classroom and end-of-course assessments, and research-based teaching and learning tools. Founded in 1947, ETS today develops, administers, and scores more than 24 million tests annually in more than 180 countries, at over 9,000 locations worldwide.

Additional information about ETS is available at www.ets.org.

Sample Size Requirements in HLM: An Empirical Study

The Relationship Between the Sample Sizes at Each Level of a Hierarchical Model and the Precision of the Outcome Model

Sabine Meinck and Caroline Vandenplas

IEA Data Processing and Research Center, Hamburg, Germany

This report was funded by the National Center for Education Statistics under Contract No. ED-08-CO-0117 with the International Association for the Evaluation of Educational Achievement (IEA). Mention of trade names, commercial products, or organizations does not imply endorsement by the U.S. Government.

IERI Monograph Series
Issues and Methodologies in Large-Scale Assessments

Special Issue 1
Sample Size Requirements in HLM: An Empirical Study
The Relationship Between the Sample Sizes at Each Level of a Hierarchical
Model and the Precision of the Outcome Model

Sabine Meinck and Caroline Vandenplas

TABLE OF CONTENTS

LIST OF TABLES AND FIGURES

Main Text

Appendix

Acknowledgements

The authors would like to express their warmest thanks to several people who helped them to complete this project. We thank Dirk Hastedt for encouraging us to take on this study. We thank Heiko Sibberns, Leslie Rutkowski, Wolfram Schulz, Eugenio Gonzalez, and the anonymous reviewer for their thorough evaluation of the paper and their valuable feedback. We are also grateful for the help of our colleagues in the Sampling Unit and the Research and Analysis Unit at the IEA Data Processing and Research Center, who helped us with various details throughout the study. Without the generous help of these individuals, this investigation would not have been possible. Finally, we thank the National Center for Education Statistics (NCES), U.S. Department of Education, Institute of Education Sciences, for funding this research project.

Abstract

This study focused on the properties of data collected in large-scale assessments (LSA) in order to explore the relationships between sample sizes at different levels of clustered data and the sampling precision of the results derived from hierarchical linear models (HLM). A Monte Carlo simulation study was used in order to explore various population and sample conditions. The varied conditions were sample sizes of and within clusters, intraclass correlation coefficients, covariance distribution, use of sampling weights, and model complexity. As expected, the precision of all explored parameters increased as sample sizes increased. The dependency took a nonlinear format—a general observation that held true for all settings. The magnitude of the increase, and whether the effect became more pronounced as sample size increased on either of the hierarchical levels, could depend, however, on all explored sample and population conditions and could also vary across the different model parameters. In conclusion, the results showed that required sample sizes depend heavily on the parameter of interest. In particular, sampling precision differed widely for fixed model parameters versus variance estimates. For certain model parameters, the effect of how the covariance was distributed between the hierarchical levels appeared to be even more pronounced than the effect of varying sample sizes. The inclusion of sampling weights in the model decreased the sampling precision of all explored parameters consistently by approximately 10%. The model complexity had an influence on the sampling precision of all observed parameters except the residual variance. The influence thus varied according to the parameter of interest as well as the considered case of covariance distribution.

1.   Introduction

Beyond controversy is the premise that education is an important factor influencing the development of national economies worldwide (Brown & Lauder, 1996; Decker, Rice, & Moore, 1997). National assessments exploring the quality and outcomes of education systems have consequently become popular in recent decades, while accretive levels of globalization have led to education increasingly being viewed from within a broader context (Dale, 2000; Suárez-Orozco & Qin-Hilliard, 2004). These developments have heightened interest in international comparative studies of education, many of which include large-scale assessments (LSA). The increasing number of educational surveys conducted by the International Association for the Evaluation of Educational Achievement (IEA) and the Organisation for Economic Co-operation and Development (OECD) are evidence of this growing interest.[1]

When analyzing data collected in large-scale educational surveys, researchers still tend to use (or to suggest the use of) simple linear regression models (Foy & Olson, 2009; Olson, Martin, & Mullis, 2008). While the application of these models is appropriate for certain types of analyses or data structures, limitations regarding their usefulness become apparent when the data have a nested structure, that is, follow specific hierarchies (Aitkin, Anderson, & Hinde, 1981; Robinson, 1950). Simple linear regression models do not consider the effects of multiple factors on different levels of the hierarchy or on their interactions. These limitations can be avoided by using hierarchical linear modeling (HLM) (e.g., Bryk & Raudenbush, 1992; Hox, 1995; Snijders & Bosker, 1999). HLM takes the multilevel structure of a comparison problem into account and allows predictors to be introduced at different levels, thereby making it possible to study the effect of the variables at the specific level in which they occur.

HLM is usually excellently suited for analyzing data collected in educational surveys. The education systems with students embedded in classes, classes embedded in schools, schools in districts, and districts in countries display the data structure for which HLM techniques were developed. In addition, general sampling strategies in international LSA generally imply the same hierarchical approach (see, for example, Martin, Mullis, & Kennedy, 2007; Olson et al., 2008).

---

1   http://www.iea.nl; http://www.oecd.org/edu

The first stage of the approach involves, in each participating country, selecting a sample of schools and stratifying them according to certain organizational criteria (e.g., public versus private, or regions comprising different strata). The second stage sees classes and/or students sampled from within each participating school. The hierarchical data structure also opens a window into broadly defined concepts of student achievement in relation to some correlates of learning, such as socioeconomic (SES) background and school resources.

Given these advantages, it is not surprising that more and more researchers want to employ HLM analysis in this field of research. However, this desire has to be taken into account when developing the general study design of an educational assessment. Researchers need to be aware at this time of an important problem associated with designing studies suitable for multilevel modeling, namely the required sample sizes at the different levels of the hierarchy (see, for example, Maas & Hox, 2005; Scherbaum & Ferreter, 2009; Snijders & Bosker, 1999).

In recent years, a number of researchers have tried to address the problem by conducting (mostly) simulation studies with certain conditions in order to produce rules of thumb or even software that enable users to determine the optimal survey design. However, the literature available on the subject tends to be highly technical, hard to apply, and not easily procured. Most importantly, existing simulation studies are based on assumptions that do not fully apply to data collected in educational LSA, either because they fail to or only partially address the features typical of these datasets.

But what are the characteristics of typical LSA survey designs? In general, minimum sample sizes in LSA are predetermined by multiple factors, such as the requested precision of population estimates, the number of items and the item rotation design (connected to the need to have minimum response numbers per item), minimum cell assignments in cross tables, and so on. For example, most IEA surveys specify a minimum sample size of 150 schools to ensure that certain precision requirements are met. To give another example, the item rotation design applied in studies such as TIMSS[2] calls for a sample size of at least 4,000 tested students per education system because each tested student takes only one-seventh of the whole assessment (Olson et al., 2008). In this second case, the total student sample size is dictated by the item rotation design while the total cluster (school) sample size is dictated by the precision requirements and the design effect. Furthermore, cluster sampling of classes often dictates within-cluster sample sizes of about 20 to 30 individuals per cluster.

In addition, data originating from complex surveys carry weights that reflect the multiple selection probabilities of each unit, adjusted for non-response. Although general sampling designs usually aim for self-weighted samples (e.g., Joncas, 2008),[3] estimation weights always vary due to stratification, practical constraints associated with implementation of the ideal sampling design, and non-response adjustments,

---

2 Trends in International Mathematics and Science Study, conducted by IEA: http://timss.bc.edu/
3 Samples that lead to equal selection probabilities of the units of interest are called self-weighted samples.

a situation that can lead to increased sampling variance. Since the development of multilevel analysis techniques, the need to consider sampling weights when engaged in multilevel modeling, as well as the influence of that modeling on estimates, has attracted attention (albeit limited) in the literature (see, for example, Asparouhov, Muthén, & Muthén, 2006; Chantala, Blanchette, & Suchindran, 2006; Korn & Graubard, 1995; Pfeffermann, Skinner, Holmes, Goldstein, & Rabash, 1998; Rabe-Hesketh & Skrondal, 2006; Stapleton, 2002; Zaccarin & Donati, 2008). However, no mention seems to have been made in this body of work of relationships between sampling weights, the statistical precision of the models, and required sample sizes.

All these constraints suggest the desirability of an evaluation of the sample sizes required to achieve a predetermined level of precision when applying multilevel modeling oriented toward the specific structure of data collected from educational large-scale assessments. Our aim, therefore, in this paper is to extend knowledge about the association between sample sizes and precision of the estimates under varying population and sample conditions and relative to model complexity.

2. Literature Review

2.1 The Concept of Hierarchical Models and Their Use in Educational Research

Inevitably, individuals interact with their social contexts. Individuals' characteristics can thus be influenced by factors attributed to the group they belong to. For instance, students in schools without a gymnasium may not be as athletic as students in schools that have one. Also, features of groups are often driven by the individuals they contain, which means that these individuals are influenced, in turn, by the "emerged" additive feature of the group to which they belong. For example, students coming from high socioeconomic backgrounds may be more likely to attend private schools than students from lower socioeconomic backgrounds. Inversely, this characteristic of students can be descriptive of private schools. In this case, one feature (socioeconomic background) influences individuals in two dimensions (or two levels of a hierarchy), that is, the individual level and at group level. Both may influence, for example, the mathematics achievement of the students. Finally, interactions between variables on both (or even more) levels are possible and may also influence any dependent variable, for instance, achievement.

Simple linear regression models have been used—and still are used—to analyze LSA data. But these models have weaknesses. One is the underlying assumption that individuals answer independently of the cluster they belong to (Burstein, 1980; Rogosa, 1978). Another is the assumption that, in terms of magnitude and direction, relationships within each group are the same as those across groups. Ignoring the nested structure of the data can lead to aggregation bias, ecological fallacy (Cronbach, 1967; Robinson, 1950), and misestimates of the precision (Aitkin et al., 1981; Knapp, 1977). Apart from these technicalities, most linear models do not allow for analyzing the group effect on the individuals or the different effects of an explanatory variable that is group dependent. It is possible to illustrate this problem within the context of the introductory example above by investigating how much of the variability of the achievement scores in the full population can be explained by introducing socioeconomic status (SES) as a group-level effect.

To overcome the constraints of the simple regression models, researchers developed a model that takes the hierarchical structure of the data into account (Aitkin & Longford, 1986; De Leeuw & Kreft, 1986; Goldstein, 1986, Raudenbush & Bryk, 1986). This model, known as the hierarchical linear model (HLM),[4] allows analysts to investigate effects, relationships, and variability at multiple levels. It also permits different intercepts and coefficients at the various levels, thus allowing the model to fit the actual data structure more accurately (Hox, 1995, 1998; Raudenbush, 1988; Thomas & Heck, 2001).

In order to gain a very brief mathematical introduction to these features, consider a basic HLM model for any dependent micro- (or individual-) level variable Y_{ij} of the ith individual in group j with one micro-level explanatory variable x_{ij} and one macro- (or group-) level explanatory variable z_j. This can be described as follows:

$$Y_{ij} = \beta_{0j} + \beta_{1j}\, x_{ij} + R_{ij}$$

$$\text{where} \begin{cases} \beta_{0j} = \gamma_{00} + \gamma_{01}z_j + U_{0j} \\ \beta_{1j} = \gamma_{10} + \gamma_{11}z_j + U_{1j} \end{cases} \text{and} \begin{cases} R_{ij} \sim N(0,\sigma^2) \\ \begin{bmatrix} U_{0j} \\ U_{1j} \end{bmatrix} \sim N(\begin{bmatrix} 0 \\ 0 \end{bmatrix}, \begin{bmatrix} \tau_{00} & \tau_{01} \\ \tau_{01} & \tau_{11} \end{bmatrix}) \end{cases}.$$

In this equation, β_{0j} is the random intercept, β_{1j} is the random slope, and R_{ij} is the micro-level error term. Furthermore, γ_{00} is the mean intercept, γ_{01}, γ_{11}, and γ_{10} are the mean slopes at the macro-, cross-, and micro-levels, and U_{0j} and U_{1j} are the macro-level residuals. The three equations can also be combined and written in a linear form as

$$Y_{ij} = \gamma_{00} + \gamma_{01}z_j\ \gamma_{10}x_{ij} + \gamma_{11}z_jx_{ij} + U_{0j} + U_{1j} + R_{ij}.$$

A main feature of HLM is that parameters (i.e., intercepts and slopes) can be specified as being *fixed* or *random* at all levels, and the error variance/covariance matrix can take different structures. Also, if the theoretical framework of a research hypothesis suggests it, more than one predictor at each level can be introduced; or, aside from the plain effects of the predictors, interaction terms can be included. Finally, models for more than two levels can be formed (e.g., students nested within teachers, teachers nested within schools). Note, however, that the interpretation complexity of any multilevel model is closely related to the model complexity.[5] Because these matters are not the scope of this report, we do not offer further detailed explanations, but instead refer interested readers to Bryk and Raudenbush (1992), Hox (1995), Goldstein (1996), and Snijders and Bosker (1999), all of whom provide excellent introductions to the topic.

---

4   The HLM is also known as the "multilevel model" (Hox, 1995; Snijders & Bosker, 1999), "variance component model" (Longford, 1993), and "random coefficient model" (De Leeuw & Kreft, 1986).

5   Complexity in the sense used here means increasing the numbers of predictors, introducing more than two hierarchical levels, or considering random instead of fixed slopes.

Data collected in educational LSA generally follow a hierarchical structure. The reason is that such studies usually apply two-stage cluster sampling designs. This specific sampling design implements two selection steps:

1. Clusters are selected from an exhaustive list of clusters (in educational studies, clusters are generally schools);

2. Individuals are selected from inside each cluster sampled in the first stage.[6]

Although these cluster samples have one important disadvantage—a considerable decrease in the precision of the sample (Cochran, 1977; Kish, 1965; Lohr, 1999)—other important reasons make this approach the preferred option. First, it often reduces the costs of the study because it is less expensive to test, for instance, one whole class in each of 150 schools than just one student in 400 schools located countrywide.[7] Second, a simple random sample requires a complete list of all individuals in the target population (e.g., all Grade 4 students in a country), which is usually not available.

Finally, a main research interest with respect to educational LSA involves investigating how group-level variables influence individual-level variables and cross-level interactions, that is, the interaction between variables measured at different levels of the hierarchy. For example, if the relationship between mathematics achievement and the SES of a student differs in terms of the averaged SES of the schools, there is a cross-level interaction.

Although the benefits of using HLM for data analyses have rarely been a critical consideration for assessment designers,[8] many educational researchers have taken advantage of the benefits of hierarchical modeling when endeavoring to best accommodate the existing data structure (e.g., Anderson, Milford, & Ross, 2009; Baker, Goesling, & Letendre, 2002; Braun, Jenkins, & Grigg, 2006; Cheong, Fotiu, & Raudenbush, 2001; Desimone, Smith, Baker, & Ueno, 2005; Green, Camilli, & Elmore, 2006; Koretz, McCaffrey, & Sullivan, 2001; Lamb & Fullarton, 2001; Lubienski & Lubienski, 2006; Ma & McIntyre, 2005; Pong & Pallas, 2001; Rumberger, 1995; Wang, 1998; Wenglinsky, 2002).

---

6   Various international LSA incorporate yet a further sampling step: within schools, classes are selected, and within the selected classes, all students are selected or a subsample of students is selected (as in, e.g., TIMSS and the Progress in Reading Literacy Study [PIRLS]).

7   Both designs are comparably efficient (assuming a moderate intraclass correlation coefficient of about 0.3), although the total sample sizes deviate by factor 10.

8   Most LSA in education have international comparisons of population estimates and trend measurement as main focuses. Study designs are mainly driven by these focuses.

2.2 Precision of the Estimates in Multilevel Models for Complex Sample Survey Data

One goal that researchers try to meet when designing a survey is to achieve a certain target level of precision for estimates of the population parameters so that they can ensure that the estimate—calculated using sample data—reflects the actual value in the population within specific margins of error.[9] Researchers may also want to detect a difference between certain groups, expose the effects of covariates, and allege interactions between different independent variables—all activities leading to conclusions that can be made only within certain confidence levels. This happens because the inference pertaining to the population is based on data collected from a sample. A measure that can be used to determine the precision of any sample estimate is the standard (or sampling) error, which allows researchers to calculate confidence intervals.

In general, the sampling error is a monotonic decreasing function of the sample size (Snijders & Bosker, 1999), and it is further affected by population variance. If complex sampling designs are applied, additional factors influence the sampling error. First, data collected from clusters are not independent. For example, students within a class are more alike than students from different classes because all members of the former group receive the same tuition from a teacher. A measure that illustrates this effect is the intraclass correlation coefficient (ICC). It displays the ratio of the between-group variability to the total variability and ranges from 0 to 1 (Kish, 1965). During estimation of sampling error for complex samples (assuming simple random sampling), sampling error estimates become downwardly biased as ICCs increase. To overcome this obstacle, sampling errors are estimated using repeated replication methods such as Jackknife Repeated Replication or Balanced Repeated Replication. This use is very common in educational LSA (e.g., Olson et al., 2008. Organisation for Economic Co-operation and Development [OECD], 2006, 2009).

Reference to an extreme example illustrates the meaning of the ICC and its effect on precision. Imagine that all students within different classes are identical, but that students from different classes differ from one another (ICC = 1). We will not obtain any further information about the population if we sample more students within the selected classes. In other words, the precision will not increase as sample sizes within clusters increase.

Multilevel models reduce the impact of ICC on the precision of the parameter and sampling error estimates. Maas and Hox (2005) report, for example, that starting with ICCs larger than 0.1 produces biased estimated parameters and sampling errors only when fewer than 30 clusters are sampled. Nevertheless, intraclass correlation

---

9   In the literature, most authors use the term "standard error" instead of "sampling error." In many circumstances, both terms have identical meaning. However, LSA often use the plausible value technique for (at least) their main outcome variables (see Von Davier, Gonzalez, & Mislevy, 2009). In these instances, the standard error captures two sources of variation—sampling error and measurement error. The measurement error is not a focus of this research. To avoid confusion, we consistently use the term "sampling error" throughout this report.

continues to be specified as one important factor influencing the quality of estimation (Asparouhov & Muthén, 2006; Asparouhov et al., 2006) and should therefore be taken into account.

Although Scherbaum and Ferreter (2009) report that the estimation of ICCs a priori (i.e., before the actual survey is done) is difficult, this is not true for most educational LSA. This is because excellent data sources are available for many participating countries from which to estimate ICCs reliably. These sources include databases from previous cycles of a survey, or surveys with similar subjects or similar target populations. Many of these databases are publicly available.[10] Note, however, that ICCs vary from one variable to the next and may vary across survey cycles.

In summary, sampling errors within multilevel models are no longer simple monotonic functions of the total sample size. As a general rule, the higher the ICC, the less the increase in precision if the sample size within clusters is increased. We review this aspect in more detail in Section 2.3.

As we have already mentioned, educational LSA require implementation of complex sampling designs. Weights reflect multiple sampling steps, selection probabilities, and non-response at each sampling stage. The use of sampling weights for estimating population parameters is a well-established procedure (see, for example, Cochran, 1977). If the probabilities of selection are ignored, the parameter estimates can be substantially biased. In most cases, the use of weighted data also affects sampling errors. Despite these occurrences, the use of sampling weights in HLM analysis has only recently been addressed in the literature.

Among those who have discussed the biased parameter estimates that occur when standard multilevel modeling without weights is used are Korn and Graubard (2003), Longford (1996), Pfeffermann et al. (1998), and Rabe-Hesketh and Skrondal (2006). Asparouhov et al. (2006) provide a discussion of the different methods of normalizing sampling weights and their impact on parameter estimation. They also offer guidelines on how to scale weights under specific conditions. Chantala et al. (2006) provide programs in Stata and SAS that allow computation of correctly scaled weights for multilevel modeling of complex survey data. Zaccarin and Donati (2008) evaluate the influence of different choices of sampling weights in HLM on PISA results.[11]

Pfeffermann, Moura, and Silva (2006) suggest a model-based approach instead of probability weighting under informative sampling designs. They found that their approach outperformed probability weighting under certain conditions in a simulation study but admitted that the latter approach is far easier to implement and needs significantly less computational power.

Finally, the inclusion of covariates at either level can influence the precision of multilevel models. This is because of their potential to reduce the between-group variance (Raudenbush, 1997; Reise & Duan, 2003).

---

10 For example, all databases from previous cycles of TIMSS and PIRLS can be downloaded at http://timssandpirls.bc.edu/ or from www.iea.nl, together with all technical documentation and user guides.

11 Programme for International Student Assessment, conducted by the OECD: http://www.pisa.oecd.org/

2.3   Sample Size Requirements and HLM—Knowledge at Hand

A general problem associated with applying any method designed to define optimal sample sizes[12] is that the sample sizes optimal for, say, the estimation of a population parameter might not be optimal for the test of, for example, a cross-level interaction effect. As Snijders and Bosker (1999) aptly point out, the fact that optimality depends on one's objectives is a general problem of life that cannot be solved by reference to a textbook.

Over the past 15 or so years, several research projects, many of which are simulation studies, have endeavored to address the issue. Only a few studies have examined the impact of various factors on statistical precision and sample sizes in hierarchical models as well as their interactions. We review the most important of these studies below.

Snijders and Bosker (1993) developed approximation formulas to calculate optimal sample sizes on two-level designs for fixed regression coefficients. They evaluated their work as being valid for sample sizes with more than 10 units on both levels. Applying their formulas to an example, a consideration of budget constraints, they showed that if small sampling errors of regression coefficients are to be achieved, then higher sample sizes at the macro-level are always preferable to increasing the sample sizes within clusters. Sampling errors increase if the number of sampled clusters decreases. This situation holds true if the total sample size is kept constant, and even when the total sample size increases. Snijders and Bosker's example also makes clear that the sampling errors of the regression coefficient of a macro-level effect are much more sensitive to sample sizes than are interaction effects between two different macro-level variables.

Afshartous (1995) addressed the topic of estimation bias in hierarchical modeling due to small samples. He showed that necessary sample sizes of micro- and macro-level units respectively vary depending on whether the interest is mainly in obtaining accurate and reliable estimates for variance components or for fixed effects. He found, in a specified setting, that 320 schools were needed in order to obtain unbiased estimates of variance components, whereas as few as 40 schools appeared to suffice for estimation of regression coefficients. However, Afshartous admitted that this effect might depend on the type of fixed effect being studied (e.g., intercept or slope). Also, Afshartous used only one specific dataset for his research (NELS13) and analyzed clearly delimited subsamples of the base dataset.

In a very thorough study, Mok (1995) investigated samples of students derived from a real dataset pertaining to 50 schools. She set a fixed total sample size, let the number of schools and students within schools vary, and then considered a variety of estimators, including regression coefficients, variances, and covariances. In agreement with other authors, she found that designs using more schools and fewer students are more

---

12 Here, "optimal sample size" refers to a sample size that will meet certain precision requirements.

13 National Educational Longitudinal Survey, U.S. Department of Education.

efficient than designs that allocate sample sizes the other way around. Based on her review of simulation studies, Kreft (1996) offered a 30/30 rule of thumb, leading to a minimum total sample size of 900, no matter what type of effect is studied. Bell, Morgan, Schoeneberger, Loudermilk, Kromrey, and Ferron (2010) have since argued against this viewpoint, claiming that this commonly cited rule would likely not yield high levels of statistical power for the fixed effects at both levels of the model.

Raudenbush (1997) made clear the fact that inclusions of covariates have an impact on the optimal design. Covariates are non-negligible because they explain substantive parts of the variance of the dependent variable. According to Raudenbush, the explanatory power of the covariate at each level becomes highly relevant for choosing optimal sample sizes. Raudenbush also focused in his paper on the efficiency of cluster randomized trials and considered cost implications. Snijders (2006) added to this aspect by observing that the reduction in sampling error depends on the intraclass correlation of the dependent variable and on the within-group and the between-group residual correlation between the dependent variable and the covariate.

Moerbeek, Van Breukelen, and Berger (2000) have also described how to allocate sample sizes to the macro- and micro-level in a cluster-randomized trial. The authors considered different treatments and budget constraints, and aimed for specified levels of power with regard to treatment effects. In another article, these authors again investigated this topic, but this time their focus was on binary outcome variables (Moerbeek, Van Breukelen, & Berger, 2001).

Cohen (1998) implemented an approach similar to that of Snijders and Bosker's (1993). He reported that the estimation of micro-level variances requires larger samples within clusters (and hence fewer clusters, assuming a fixed cost budget) than does estimation of traditional quantities, such as means, totals, and ratios.

Hox (1995) provided another rule of thumb. He advocated sample sizes of 50 clusters and 20 individuals per cluster as appropriate for multilevel modeling.

Maas and Hox (2005) carried out a simulation study with varying numbers of clusters (N = 30, 50, 100), varying cluster sizes (n = 5, 30, 50), and varying intraclass correlations (ICC = 0.1, 0.2, 0.3) in order to explore the effect of these variations on parameter estimates and estimates of their sampling errors. The authors found that the regression coefficients and variance components were all estimated with negligible bias (using restricted maximum likelihood as the estimation method). Also, sampling errors for regression coefficients were estimated correctly. However, the authors stated that sampling error estimates of macro-level variances were downwardly biased when the number of clusters was substantially lower than 100 (i.e., 50 or 30 in their study).

Snijders (2005) took a more general approach when addressing the topic. He pointed out that the sample size at the micro-level (i.e., the total sample size) matters if the effect of a micro-level variable is of main interest, and (vice versa) that the sample size on the macro-level is more important when testing a main effect of a macro-level variable. He concluded that, in most instances, a sample with more macro-level units will be more informative than a sample where the within-cluster sample size is enlarged but fewer clusters are selected. He also explained that small cluster sizes are unproblematic when testing regression coefficients but have a negative impact on test power when testing random slope variances at the macro-level. Snijders gives, in line with suggestions made during an earlier work (Snijders & Bosker, 1999), some formulas that can be used to obtain insight into the design aspects that are most influential on power and sampling errors. Both sources indicate that the formulas will give only very rough estimates of the required sample sizes if several correlated explanatory variables, some of which will have random slopes, are to be introduced in the model.

Okumura (2007) presented a new simulation-based approach to determine optimal sample sizes for HLM that lead to desired levels of statistical power and mean ranges of confidence intervals. Specifically, his method acknowledges uncertainty in parameter values, given the posterior distribution for the unknown parameters. Okumura cited, as disadvantages of his approach, the fact that the method takes much more computational time than existing techniques and that it is very difficult to adapt computer programs to meet specific model conditions.

Finally, various computer programs are available that enable users to conduct power estimations under specific conditions. The two programs that serve modules closest to the object of our interest are PinT[14] and OD.[15]

PinT (*Power in Two-level designs*) calculates sampling errors of regression coefficients in two-level designs as a function of fixed total-sample sizes. It also takes into account cost constraints. According to Snijders and Bosker (1999), the greatest difficulty in using this software is that means, variances, and covariances of all explanatory variables and random effects have to be specified. Furthermore, the program uses relatively rough, large sample approximations to obtain sampling errors.

The other program, OD (*Optimal Design*), calculates power and optimal sample sizes for testing treatment effects and variance components in multisite and cluster-randomized trials with balanced two-group designs, and in repeated-measurement designs (Raudenbush, Spybrook, Liu, & Congdon, 2005). Because LSA are generally observational surveys rather than experimental ones, this program is another that does not fully fit the needs of sample-size calculations for these assessments.

---

14 With manual available for free download at http://stat.gamma.rug.nl/multilevel.htm#progPINT

15 With manual available for free download at http://sitemaker.umich.edu/group-based/optimal_design_software

2.4   Cost Implications of Sample Size Considerations

All decisions pertaining to sample sizes have cost implications. Many authors have therefore addressed this issue in their research and tried to optimize sample size to accommodate budget constraints (e.g., Cohen, 1998; Moerbeek et al., 2000, 2001; Mok, 1995; Snijders & Bosker, 1993, 1999).

Cost reductions are often obvious and significant when fewer macro-level units need to be selected for a survey because, in most cases, it is more expensive to survey one more cluster than one more individual within each cluster. However, reducing micro-level sample sizes could also have significant cost implications in certain circumstances. This effect will typically show up in surveys that do not have predetermined micro-level sample sizes.[16] These surveys are often those carried out with non-student target populations. Inservice teachers in ICCS[17] and TALIS[18] and future teachers in their final year of training and their educators in TEDS-M[19] provide examples of these populations. With these surveys, the decision to select, for instance, 15 or 20 teachers from a total of 150 schools does indeed matter because the need for high participation rates often makes necessary considerable engagement with personnel or the setting of incentives, such as payments. Faced with limited budgets, researchers need to focus on securing optimal survey designs that have minimum cost implications.

---

16 In student surveys, full classrooms are often surveyed. In these cases, the within-cluster sample size is predetermined.

17 International Civic and Citizenship Education Survey, conducted by IEA: http://iccs.acer.edu.au/

18 Teaching and Learning International Survey, conducted by OECD: http://www.oecd.org/edu/talis

19 Teacher Education and Development Study in Mathematics, conducted by IEA: http://teds.educ.msu.edu/

3. Research Questions

The literature review shows that knowledge about how best to determine sample sizes when using multilevel modeling for data analysis is still developing. During our literature review, we could not find any definite or generalized solutions regarding this matter. Also, many of the authors we reviewed indicated that relying solely on the simulation studies in place may be inadvisable.

What we did find from the available literature was that those researchers who suggest sample sizes for studies that will use HLM for data analysis either do not or only partially consider the specific conditions of typical educational LSA, such as the complex sample design with unequal selection probabilities and specific predetermined sample sizes.[20] Also, the typical values of ICCs for the usual main outcome variables (student achievement in, for instance, mathematics, science, or reading) are higher in educational LSA than are the values considered in most of the reviewed articles. We furthermore could find very little evidence of work intent on exploring the connection between sample sizes and random slopes.

These reasons validate the contribution of the presented research, during which we endeavored to answer the following research questions:

- What is the association between sample sizes at each level of a two-level hierarchy[21] and the precision of the estimated model parameters when applying HLM analysis within the context of the specific features of data collected in LSA?
- What influences do the varying population conditions (specifically, intraclass correlation coefficients and covariance distributions) have on the sampling errors of the model parameters?
- Do varying selection probabilities of the clusters and the model complexity have an influence on these results?

---

20 Many studies at hand deal with cluster sample sizes below 100. Most educational LSA, however, predetermine significantly larger samples.

21 A two-level hierarchy was chosen because it reflects a typical sampling setting in educational studies, with schools (or classes) and students as hierarchical levels.

Tables and graphs showing the relationships between sample sizes and the precision of the results in specific hierarchical models, to the extent to which they depend on the sampling error,[22] are the outcomes of this research. The information contained in this material should enable researchers to optimize, in a straightforward way, sampling precision within their respective study designs. This information should also enable researchers conducting secondary analysis of available LSA datasets to evaluate, in advance, the precision range that they can expect—with respect to their research questions—from the data. As an important side-effect, the survey design can also be optimized in terms of cost, given that adaptations of sample sizes at different levels of the hierarchy always have cost implications. We consider, in our exploration of these conditions, the specifics of data collected in educational LSA.

---

22 The measurement error and the dependency of the model accuracy on the applied estimation method are not the subject of this research. Interested readers should consult Wu (2010) for further information on error terms in LSA.

4.   Data and Methods

In order to answer the research questions, we conducted a simulation study based on the structure of IEA LSA data. Application of Monte Carlo simulation allowed us to draw samples with specific designs from an infinite population with particular features. For each specified scenario, we created 6,000 sample replicates. All samples displayed a two-level cluster design and mimicked the structure and particulars of typical datasets originating from educational surveys, that is, students nested in schools.[23] We then analyzed all sample replicates with four different two-level hierarchical linear models. The sampling errors—and therefore the precision—of all model parameters derived from 6,000 replicates can be regarded as outcomes of this research. We also examined the dependency of the sampling errors on varying sample designs (sample sizes at the student level and the school level, consideration of sampling weights) and on population parameters (i.e., the intraclass correlation and covariance structure).

4.1   Fixed Population and Sample Parameters

The data used to produce all outcomes were obtained from Monte Carlo simulations. We describe the different sampling scenarios in Section 4.2 below. The 6,000 sample replicates per scenario were selected from an infinite population that had the following characteristics:

- A two-level hierarchical structure, with individuals (e.g., students) at Level 1 and clusters (e.g., schools[24]) at Level 2;

- A normally distributed variable with a mean of 500 and a standard deviation of 100 to represent students' academic achievement;

---

23 Note that in many LSA whole classrooms are selected within schools (e.g., TIMSS, PIRLS, ICCS) instead of students selected across classrooms (e.g., PISA). In the former case, Level 2 is built up by the class rather than the school, or, more specifically, clustering effects come from both the school and the class level. However, the two effect levels cannot be disentangled using a three-level hierarchical model because the number of classes sampled per school—and even the number of classes available in each school—is clearly too small to allow setting up a meaningful respective model. Consequently, we decided not to address the disentangling effects from schools versus classes in our research.

24 Because this research mimics real hierarchical models applied in educational research, we use the terms "school" and "cluster" interchangeably in the text.

- The total variance of the achievement variable fixed at 10,000. The distribution of this variable into between-cluster (Level 2, schools) and within-cluster (Level 1, students) variance was determined by the considered ICC of the achievement variable (see Section 4.2.2). For instance, if the intraclass correlation coefficient was set to 0.1, then the within-cluster variance would be 9,000 and the between-cluster variance 1,000;

- A normally distributed variable with a mean of 0 and a standard deviation of 1 to reflect student SES;

- The within-cluster variance of the SES indicator set to 0.7 and the between cluster variance set to 0.3; and

- The covariance between the SES indicator and the achievement variable set to 30, which meant that the correlation between these two variables was 0.3.[25]

The decisions that we made when determining these parameters were based on the results of preliminary simulations and/or examination of TIMSS and PISA data, as described in the following sections.

4.1.1 Number of replicates

When investigating HLM model parameter estimation, several researchers have either repeatedly selected subsamples from a base sample with known properties or used a Monte Carlo simulation. These researchers include, amongst others, Maas and Hox (2005), Muthén and Muthén (2002), and Okumura (2007); refer also to Section 2.3.

In the current study, we examined a setting with fixed sample sizes (150 clusters, 10 individuals per cluster) in order to determine the number of sample replicates needed. The sampling errors of the parameters of Models 1 and 2 (see Section 4.3) were estimated for increasing numbers of replicates (1,000 to 30,000) and varying ICCs. With roughly 6,000 replicates (or with fewer numbers of replicates), the estimates of the sampling error stabilized sufficiently for all considered model parameters.

4.1.2 Achievement variable scale and socioeconomic status indicator

Most publicly available educational LSA datasets use an achievement outcome variable scaled to have a mean of 500 and a standard deviation of 100, as is the case with TIMSS, PIRLS,[26] ICCS,[27] TEDS, and PISA. It therefore seemed appropriate to adopt the same distribution for the achievement variable in the present study.

PISA provides an SES indicator with a mean of 0 and a standard deviation of 1 (OECD, 2006; Schulz, 2006). Also, many researchers drawing on other educational datasets have used a similar scale to calculate this indicator (Caro & Lehmann, 2009; Caro, McDonald, & Willms, 2009; Willms, 2003; Willms & Shields, 1996). We therefore used the same distribution for the SES indicator.

---

25 The correlation between two variables is equal to the covariance between these two variables, divided by the product of their standard deviations (in this case, $30/[100*1] = 0.3$).

26 Progress in International Reading Literacy Study, conducted by IEA: http://pirls.bc.edu/

27 International Civics and Citizenship Study, conducted by IEA: http://www.iea.nl/iccs_2009.html

4.1.3   Covariance between the SES indicator and the achievement variable

In order to determine a default value for the covariance between the SES indicator and the achievement variable, we examined data from TIMSS 2007 (Grade 8 population).

The SES indicator variable derived from TIMSS data was built as a composite of home possessions, mother's education, and father's education, according to the approach proposed by Caro (2010).[28] Two major methods were used to calculate this measure of SES: IRT and principal component analysis (PCA). First, a home possessions index was estimated by means of a Rasch model (Masters & Wright, 1997; Rasch, 1980). Secondly, the first principal component was used to summarize the home possessions index and mother's and father's education into the single SES index. The final SES measure was standardized to have a mean of 0 and a standard deviation of 1 for the TIMSS 2007 Grade 8 student population.

On average across the full database (which included more than 200,000 surveyed students from 53 countries), the correlation was 0.294. For 60% of the participating countries, the correlation ranged from 0.2 to 0.4. On the basis of these results, we chose a covariance of 30, which corresponds to a correlation of 0.3, as the default value of the infinite population that we used as the starting point for the Monte Carlo simulation.

4.1.4   Within- and between-schools variance of the SES indicator

We again used the TIMSS 2007 data for the Grade 8 population to examine the within- and between-school variance of the SES indicator.[29] We used the average values for the variance across the examined countries as default values for the presented research (0.7 for the within- and 0.3 for the between-school variance of the SES indicator).

4.2   Varied Population and Sample Parameters

The following subsections describe which parameters we varied in order to examine different population and sampling scenarios. Overall, we examined 288 different sampling scenarios. Table A1 in the appendix provides an overview of these scenarios.

4.2.1   Sample size of clusters and within clusters

In order to examine the effects of cluster sample sizes on sampling errors of the studied HLM models, we set the number of sampled clusters (or schools) to 50, 100, 150, and 200. These cluster sample sizes are highly relevant in educational LSA.

The minimum total school sample size is generally set to 150 per participating country in these assessments. However, certain conditions, such as the following examples, make it necessary to select larger samples.

---

28 The index for this composite measure is similar to the SES index developed for PISA (Schulz, 2006).

29 An arbitrary sample of 13 participating countries was examined: Algeria, Bulgaria, Colombia, the Czech Republic, Ghana, Hungary, Indonesia, Iran, Italy, Korea, the Russian Federation, Tunisia, and the United States.

- The minimum sample size for students cannot be achieved with 150 schools due to small average school sizes.

- Large variances between schools with respect to the main subjects of interest cause high sampling errors. In such cases, the required precision of the estimates can only be achieved by increasing sample sizes.

Because research interest often focuses on single explicit strata and because the sample size within an explicit stratum is usually much smaller than in the whole sample, we also studied cluster sample sizes of 50 and 100.

In order to examine the influences of different within-cluster sample sizes, we considered 5, 10, 15, 20, 25, and 30 individuals per cluster for each case. While the higher values (≥ 20) naturally correspond to usual within-school sample sizes of students, we considered it would be interesting to determine if smaller sample sizes would satisfy certain precision requirements on estimates as well. We kept the group sizes within one sampling scenario equal so as to simplify the model conditions.[30]

4.2.2 Intraclass correlation coefficients (ICCs)

Intraclass correlation coefficients for student populations tend to range from 0.1 to 0.4. These values can be derived from publicly available LSA datasets, such as those from the various cycles of TIMSS and PISA. Only on rare occasions are higher coefficients found in the data from the different participating countries. We therefore set the ICC levels to be examined to 0.1, 0.2, 0.3, and 0.4.

4.2.3 Distribution of covariance between the SES indicator and the achievement variable between the hierarchical levels

As we explained in Section 4.1.3, we set the overall covariance of the SES indicator and the achievement variable to 30. Two different distributions of the covariance over Level 1 and Level 2 were considered in this study. In the first case, the covariance was determined to be stronger at the within level (covariance = 20 within and 10 between clusters). In the second case, the covariance was determined to be stronger at the between level (covariance = 10 within and 20 between clusters).

The latter case is evident with higher ICCs and is often typical for students in highly tracked education systems: the influence of SES on achievement is stronger across schools because students within schools are more similar. This second case was examined in connection with ICC levels 0.2, 0.3, and 0.4.[31] In the first case, the ICC was low: the clusters were more similar to one another but the connection between SES and achievement appeared stronger within the cluster. We examined this case in connection with ICC levels 0.1, 0.2, and 0.3.

---

30 Corrections for clustering based on the design effect assume equal group sizes (Kish, 1965); multilevel analysis does not. However, Maas and Hox (2005) found no discernible effect of unbalance on multilevel estimates or their standard errors even in extreme unbalanced designs. This outcome is also supported by work conducted by Grilli and Pratesi (2004).

31 If an ICC of 0.1 is considered, the maximum value for the covariance between clusters is 10. Therefore, this ICC could not be considered in the second case.

4.2.4   Weights

All sampling scenarios were first analyzed (see Section 4.3) using unweighted data. As we pointed out in the literature review, LSA data are usually collected from surveys with complex sampling designs. This means that individuals and clusters may have different selection probabilities. Data collected by means other than a simple random sample should therefore be analyzed with caution. If the complexity of the sample designs is overlooked, the estimates can be severely biased. Rutkowski, Gonzalez, Joncas, and von Davier (2010) outline the correct use of sampling weights in hierarchical modeling of data drawn from LSA.

In order to achieve self-weighted samples in LSA,[32] the primary sampling units (here, schools/clusters) are generally selected with probabilities proportional to their sizes (see, in this regard, Joncas, 2008). This selection method results in school design weights that follow the character of a Poisson distribution.[33] Figure 4.1 illustrates this fact with regard to the TIMSS 2007 Grade 8 population. Because the base weights of Level 1 units (here, students) in many LSA are all identical within a cluster, we disregarded them in this research. Consequently, we created Level 2 design weights as random variables that followed a Poisson distribution:

$$f(k,\lambda) = \frac{\lambda^k e^{-\lambda}}{k!}.$$

Here, $\lambda = 2$ and k is a positive integer, attached to all 6,000 datasets in each of the 288 different sampling scenarios. We analyzed all sampling scenarios a second time, using weighted data.

4.3   Hierarchical Models

We analyzed, for each sample scenario, four different hierarchical models, each of which we describe below. In order to bring meaning to the abstract equations, we provide an exemplary research question for each model.

- *Model 1—the empty (or null) model:* This model does not contain an explanatory variable and the intercept is random.

$$\begin{cases} y = \beta_0 + \varepsilon \\ \beta_0 = \gamma_{00} + U_0 \end{cases} \tag{1}$$

Example research question: To what extent are students within schools more alike than students between schools in terms of their academic achievement?

The question could be answered by measuring, as an outcome of this model, the intraclass correlation coefficient of a given country.

---

32 Study targets have similar estimation weights.

33 Weights are inversely proportional to the selection probability. The sampling method applied in most LSA (sampling with selection probabilities proportional to size) leads to similar distributions of selection probabilities (and consequently weights), as evident with Poisson sampling (see, for example, Sarndal, Swenson, & Wretman, 1992).

Figure 4.1: Distribution of design weights of schools (over all participating countries, after z-transformation at country level)

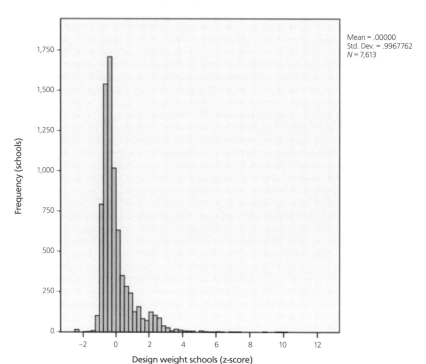

Source: TIMSS 2007, Grade 8.

• *Model 2:* This model has one explanatory variable at Level 1. The intercept is random and the slope is fixed.

$$\begin{cases} y = \beta_0 + \beta_1 x_{ij} + \varepsilon \\ \quad \beta_0 = \gamma_{00} + U_0 \\ \quad\quad \beta_1 = \gamma_{10} \end{cases}$$

(2)

Example research question: What is the association between family SES and academic achievement at the individual level, after controlling for school-level effects?

This association can be measured by β_1 and its significance.

- *Model 3:* Here, there is one explanatory variable at Level 1 and one explanatory variable at Level 2. The intercept is random and the slope is fixed.

$$\begin{cases} y = \beta_0 + \beta_1 x_{ij} + \varepsilon \\ \beta_0 = \gamma_{00} + \gamma_{01} x_j + U_0 \\ \quad \beta_1 = \gamma_{10} \end{cases}$$

(3)

Example research question: Is there evidence for contextual SES influences?

Or, what is the difference in academic achievement between two students with comparable SES levels but who attend schools that differ in terms of school SES?

This can be captured by γ_{01} when x_{ij} is the individual SES variable and x_j is the averaged school SES. γ_{01} captures contextual effects if SES at Level 1 is grand-mean centered. If the mean is group centered, then contextual effects are approximated by $\gamma_{01} - \gamma_{10}$.

- *Model 4:* This model has one explanatory variable at Level 1 and one explanatory variable at Level 2. The intercept and the slope are random.

$$\begin{cases} y = \beta_0 + \beta_1 x_{ij} + \varepsilon \\ \beta_0 = \gamma_{00} + \gamma_{01} x_j + U_0 \\ \quad \beta_1 = \gamma_{10} + U_1 \end{cases}$$

(4)

Example research question: Does the influence of SES on achievement vary between schools, that is, does SES affect students' achievement in different schools to different magnitudes or even directions?

This construct is measured by U_1 and its significance.

For each model, the variables are defined as:

y Achievement variable

x_{ij} SES indicator at Level 1

x_j SES indicator at Level 2

ε Residual variance

β_0 Random intercept

γ_{00} Mean of random intercepts

U_0 Variance of random intercepts

γ_{01} Slope of random intercepts

β_1 Fixed or random slope (SES indicator)

γ_{10} Mean of random slopes (SES indicator)

U_1 Variance of random slopes (SES indicator)

where $\begin{cases} \varepsilon \sim N(0, \sigma^2) \\ \begin{bmatrix} U_0 \\ U_1 \end{bmatrix} \sim N(\begin{bmatrix} 0 \\ 0 \end{bmatrix}, \begin{bmatrix} \tau_{00} & \tau_{01} \\ \tau_{01} & \tau_{11} \end{bmatrix}) \end{cases}$.

The hierarchical models that we chose are ones that are commonly used in educational research.

To summarize, we applied four different hierarchical models to analyze 288 different sampling scenarios, each with 6,000 replicates.

4.4 Outcomes

4.4.1 Coefficients of variation

The sampling error for each of the model parameters in the four different models was the main outcome of this research. The Monte Carlo simulation offered two possible ways of retrieving these sampling errors:[34]

1. The sampling error could be estimated as the standard deviation of the sample distribution over the 6,000 sample replicates per sample scenario. This method provides an unbiased and (given the sample size of 6,000) very reliable and precise estimate of the true sampling error. Sampling errors obtained by this method are further referred to as SE (Method I).

2. The sampling error could be estimated by using a sandwich estimator (the standard Huber-White procedure;[35] Muthén, 2008) for each sample replicate. With this method, the average of the 6,000 sampling error estimates should also provide a good estimate of the real sampling error for a given model parameter. Sampling errors obtained by this method are further referred to as SE (Method II).

As the results of our research show, the two methods gave almost identical sampling error estimates for most model parameters and under most different sampling scenarios. An example of this similarity is shown in Figure 4.2 where both lines flow almost congruently. However, the sampling error of the mean, the variance, and the slope of the random intercepts are systematically underestimated by Method II if the number of sampled clusters is small (i.e., < 100, see Figure 4.3 for an example). Note that other authors (Maas & Hox, 2005; Van der Leeden, Busing, & Meijer, 1997) report similar observations with regard to macro-level variance estimates. In addition, and to an even greater extent, the sampling error of the variance of the random slope (evaluated in Model 4) is strongly overestimated by Method II (see Figure 4.4).[36] We consequently decided to use throughout our research only those SEs estimated by Method I.[37]

---

34 See also Muthén and Muthén (2002).

35 The Huber-White sandwich estimator is calculated using a Taylor series expansion.

36 We refer interested readers to Maas and Hox (2005), who evaluated bias in the estimation of standard errors in hierarchical models under certain conditions. Also, as Muthén and Muthén (2002) point out, sampling error in hierarchical modeling might be over- or underestimated depending on the situation.

37 Although this matter is not the focus of this research, users of Mplus should be aware of the possible over/ underestimation of sampling errors of specific model parameters when exploring similar hierarchical models.

Figure 4.2: Exemplary comparison of two methods of SE estimation: Model 1, SE of residual variance, mean over four ICC levels

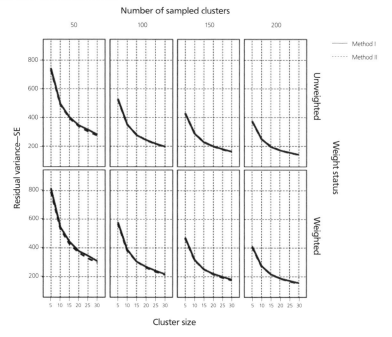

Figure 4.3: Exemplary comparison of two methods of SE estimation: Model 3, SE of slope of random intercepts, mean over two cases of covariance distribution and four ICC levels

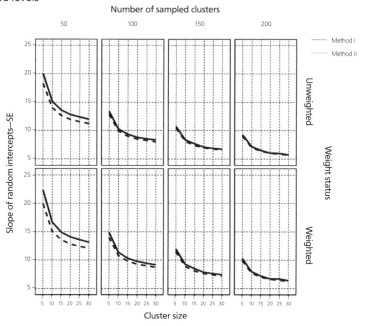

Figure 4.4: Comparison of two methods of SE estimation: Model 4, SE of variance of random slope, mean over two cases of covariance distribution and four ICC levels

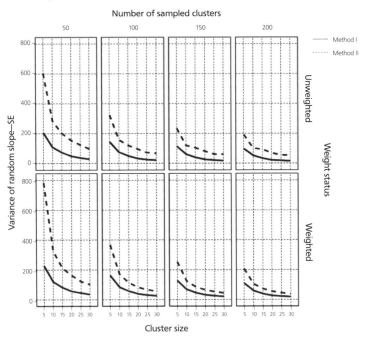

The actual value of the sampling error is meaningful only in connection to the value of the parameter for which it is calculated. For example, a sampling error of 5 has no meaning unless it is considered as the sampling error for a particular mean, say, 500. Also, we were interested not so much in the mere magnitude of the sampling errors as in the "behavior" of these errors under changing sampling conditions. Therefore, we decided to present coefficients of variation, calculated as

$$CV\,(\%) = \frac{SE\,(Parameter) \times 100}{Parameter} \qquad (5)$$

in order to display the sampling error as a percentage of the parameter it was estimated for. We used SE estimated by Method I to calculate this ratio. The following example illustrates this concept (refer also to Figure 4.5).

Consider the residual variance ε in Model 1. Not surprisingly, this parameter differs if the population is modeled with different ICCs. As can be seen in the first graph of Figure 4.5, the value of the residual variance differs by 1,000 across the four different ICC levels. The value does not differ, however, according to the number of sampled clusters or their size. If the effect of the ICCs on the sampling error is considered by merely examining the sheer value of the sampling error, one may conclude wrongly that the behavior of the SE of the residual variance depends on the ICC level (shown in the second graph of Figure 4.5). But this is not the case if we consider instead the proportion between the parameter itself and its SE. As is evident in the third graph in

Figure 4.5, the lines for the different ICC levels flow congruently, which means that the ICC level has no influence on the SE of the residual variance.

The ratio can also be used to determine if a specific parameter is significant: dividing the respective coefficient by its sampling error gives the respective t statistic. For example, if the coefficient of variation is 40% and the coefficient has a value of 50, its sampling error will be 20 and the t-value will equal 2.5, which would be considered significantly different from zero.[38]

Figure 4.5: Residual variance, its SE and the CV (%) (y-axes) by cluster size (x-axes): Model 1, average over all sampling scenarios

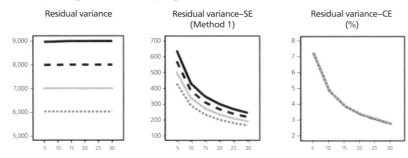

Note: The different lines display different ICC levels.

4.4.2   Curve estimation and equations

A glance at the graphs displayed above suggests that the curves describing the coherence between coefficients of variation and the different sample scenario settings seem to follow a curvilinear course. In fact, fitting quadratic functions to the curves arose as the best method of describing any of the outcome curves mathematically.[39] For most of these quadratic regression models, the R squares are above 0.95, which means that the equations fit the curves extremely well. Therefore, for each setting, we fitted a quadratic function and made cluster sample sizes and number of clusters the independent variables, thereby producing this format:

$$y = b_0 + b_1 z + b_2 z^2. \tag{6}$$

Here, y is the coefficient of variation of the explored model parameter, b are the estimated curve parameters, and z is the cluster sample size or the number of clusters.

We could argue that the curves might be better described as exponential functions because a quadratic function (with a negative slope) would have a fixed minimum and would then increase (which is counter-intuitive). However, exponential equations did not fit the curves as well as quadratic ones—R^2 was smaller for exponential equations. We do acknowledge, though, that the equations should not be used outside the ranges of the explored sample sizes and population conditions.

---

38 Given sufficient degrees of freedom and a significance level of $p < 0.05$.

39 Afshartous (1995) explored the dependency of sampling errors on different sampling settings for hierarchical models with fixed effects. He mentioned that there is a "somewhat" quadratic connection between the Level 2 sample size and the sampling errors.

The claim of describing the coherence between coefficients of variation and the different sample scenario settings by quadratic functions receives support from the findings of other researchers. Cohen (1998) and Longford (1993) described the maximum likelihood estimates of variance components (parameters ε, U_0, and U_1) of hierarchical models as having asymptotic sampling variances.[40] Cohen (1998), for example, displayed estimated sampling variances of school-level variance components depending on the within-cluster sample size (see Figure 4.6). As the sample within clusters exceeds 20, the curve does indeed increase. So, what we see in our explored conditions might be only the first part of such a function, which does follow a quadratic course.

Figure 4.6: Estimated variance of the school-level variance component by within-cluster sample size

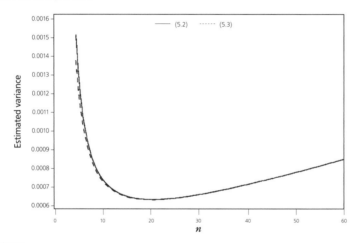

Note:
The school-level variance component in our models is parameter U_0. See Cohen (1998, p. 272).

The equations resulting from the curve estimations appear in the appendix. In addition to the curve parameters, the appendix tables contain goodness-of-fit measures (R^2) and p-values. (In Section 5.3, we explain in detail how to use these equations in order to retrieve required sample sizes for practical use.) The appendix tables are also accompanied by figures (Appendix Figures 1 to 41) that give diagrammatic form to the equations.[41]

Researchers interested in including the sample sizes for both levels in the equations can do so fairly easily by replacing the terms b_0, b_1, and b_2 in Equation (6) by other quadratic terms derived from the displayed equations. We decided not to conduct this step in order to keep the results simple and "user friendly."

---

40 The sampling error is the square root of the sampling variance.

41 Readers should assume that reference to the appendix tables includes references to the figures accompanying the tables.

Application of the relevant equation makes it possible to estimate the expected coefficient of variation of the respective model parameter under specific sampling conditions. Or, in turn, the minimum sample size can be derived by solving the equation for z if certain precision levels are required. The graphs can be utilized similarly, providing the requested information in a more handy way, but offering less precision.

4.5   Software Used

Although many statistical packages exist that provide tools for the appropriate analysis of multilevel data (e.g., HLM, SAS, MLwiN), we chose the statistical software package Mplus (Muthén & Muthén, 2008) to create all replicated datasets and to conduct the HLM analyses. Our choice was based on two main reasons. First, Mplus can be used as a powerful tool for Monte Carlo simulation. This is because the software makes it possible to automate the selection of subsamples from a predetermined artificial population with specific features. Secondly, the HLM tool of the software enables users to apply sampling weights and to use PML (pseudo maximum likelihood)[42] as a contemporary method of parameter estimation that is approximately unbiased.[43] In short, most of the steps described above can be performed within a single software package.

We used SAS 9.1 to create weights as random variables following a Poisson distribution. We used the graphic tool PASW 1.0 to develop the presented figures.

---

42 If Level 1 units are selected with unequal selection probabilities at the second sampling stage, an extended method—MPML (multilevel pseudo maximum likelihood)—is applied in Mplus (Mutthén & Muthén, 2008).

43 The currently available estimation methods are called "approximately unbiased" because various simulation studies indicate that parameter estimates can be biased, especially if cluster sample sizes are small (Graubard & Korn, 1996; Korn & Graubard, 2003; Pfeffermann et al., 1998, 2006; Stapleton, 2002). The results of our research, during which we used PML as the estimation method, support these findings.

5. Results and Discussion

5.1 Coefficients of Variation of the Different Models' Parameters

In this chapter, we display and discuss the dependency of the sampling errors of the different parameters on varying sampling and population conditions. This dependency sometimes differs according to varying conditions and from one explored model to the next. Obviously, not every parameter is part of all four models. Table 5.1 provides an overview of the explored parameters, their model allocation, and whether they were measured between or within clusters.

Note here that the displayed graphs throughout this chapter depict only a purposive sample of the results obtained from the study and that we have illustrated only the most interesting findings graphically. The structure of the graphs therefore varies according to the message each needs to convey. Further associations are displayed graphically in the appendix.

Table 5.1: Explored model parameters and their model allocation*

Parameter	Notation of parameter	Parameter is estimated in ...				Parameter is estimated ...	
		Model 1	Model 2	Model 3	Model 4	Between clusters	Within clusters
Residual variance	ε	X	X	X	X		X
Mean of random x intercepts	γ_{00}	X	X	X	X	X	
Variance of random intercepts	U_0	X	X	X	X	X	
Fixed slope	β_1		X	X			X
Slope of random intercepts	γ_{01}			X	X	X	
Mean of random slopes	γ_{10}				X	X	
Variance of random slopes	U_1				X	X	

Note: * Refer to Chapter 4.3 for definitions of the four models.

5.1.1   Residual variance

The residual variance in the hierarchical models represents the part of the total variance attributed to the within-group level. As already mentioned and graphically demonstrated in Section 4.4.1, the residual variance itself varies with the ICC but its coefficient of variation does not. The association between the coefficient of variation of the residual variance and the sample sizes on both levels, and whether the data were weighted or not, turned out to be completely independent of the type of model explored and of the covariance case being considered. The relationship is shown in Figure 5.1.

Figure 5.1: CV (%) of the residual variance by weight status and sample size at both levels

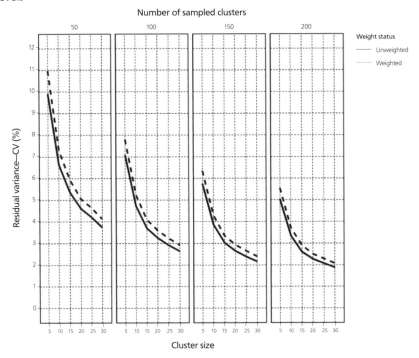

Clearly, the coefficient of variation increased exponentially as sample sizes on both levels decreased. Because the parameter is measured at the within-cluster level, only the increase of the total sample size matters; the level on which it is increased is less relevant. For example, selection of 100 clusters of size 20 results in the same error margins as selection of 200 clusters of size 10, a fact that could have relevance for cost discussions.

Overall, the sampling error assumed relatively low proportions compared with the sampling error of other model parameters, particularly other parameters measuring variances (explored in the sections below). Hence, the residual variance is a model parameter that can be estimated with comparatively high precision, even when the sample sizes are small.

Weights also had a slight but obvious enlarging effect on the coefficient of variation of the parameter of interest. Comparison of the coefficients of variation of unweighted and weighted data showed the latter increasing by a factor of 1.1 on average over the different settings. Note, however, that this effect decreased slightly with increasing sample sizes, on both Levels 1 and 2.

Tables A2 and A3 in the appendix provide the quadratic regression equations fitted to the displayed curves.

5.1.2 Mean of random intercepts

Introducing a random intercept in a model acknowledges the possibility that all clusters have their own mean. The term γ_{00} is the mean over the different group means.

Figures 5.2 and 5.3 show the dependency of the coefficient of variation of the mean of random intercepts (parameter γ_{00}) on the varied sample and population parameters. In general, we can see that the precision of this parameter is very high. Across all different sampling settings, the coefficient of variation of this parameter ranges from 0.4% to 2.2%. In fact, this parameter was the one that could be measured with the highest precision in all models.

Figure 5.2: CV (%) of the mean of random intercepts by weight status, ICC, and sample size at both levels: Models 1 and 2

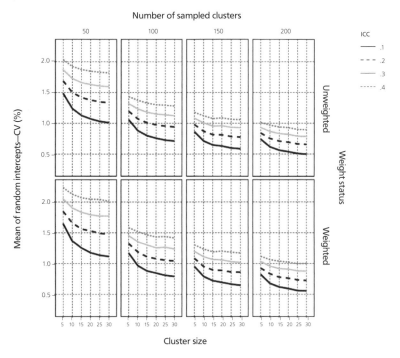

Figure 5.3: CV (%) of the mean of random intercepts by covariance distribution, ICC, and sample size at both levels: Models 3 and 4, unweighted data

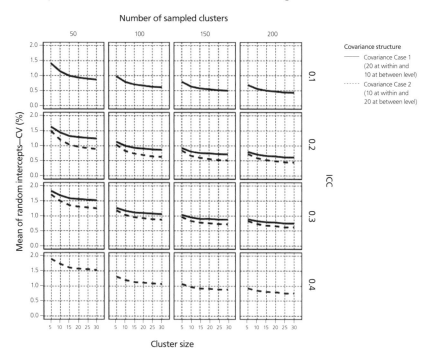

As sample sizes increased, the coefficient of variation decreased, with the decrease following the format of a quadratic function within the explored ranges. This held true for the sample sizes on both levels. Also evident here is the fact that this parameter can be measured with much higher precision if—assuming constant total-sample sizes—the Level 2 sample size is favored over the Level 1 sample size. For example, if the total sample size is 500, the coefficient of variation is smaller when 100 clusters, each of size 5, are sampled than when 50 clusters, each of size 10, are sampled. This pattern aligns with findings from various authors (e.g., Cohen, 1998; Mok, 1995; Snijders, 2005).

Introducing weights and increasing ICC levels induced higher sampling errors. On average over the different settings, weights enlarged the coefficients of variation by a factor of 1.1 to 1.2, while increasing ICCs enlarged the coefficients of variation by up to 0.2%, stepping from one ICC level to the next.

The same effect of the ICC on sampling errors of population total means is well known. For example, the PISA technical report (OECD, 2006) illustrates the relationship between ICC and sampling errors of mean estimates, here dependent on total sample sizes. The more similar the individuals are within clusters (high ICC), the less precise the estimates are, assuming the sample size is stable. However, according to our findings, the effect of the ICC on the coefficient of variation of γ_{00} amplified with increasing within-cluster sample sizes but it remained stable for increasing Level 2 sample sizes. This can be seen by comparing the graphs in Figure 5.2 above with Figure A4 in the appendix: the gaps between the lines widen as cluster sizes increase (Figure 5.2), but they barely widen as the numbers of sampled clusters increase (Figure A4, appendix).

The relationship between the coefficient of variation of the explored parameter and the sample settings was uniform for Models 1 and 2. For these two models, the considered cases of covariance distribution had no influence on this relationship.[44] Figure 5.2 depicts the explored association graphically for the first two models. The respective quadratic equations estimated to describe the curves can be found in Tables A4 and A5 of the appendix.

The Figure 5.2 graph makes it possible to easily reconstruct the general minimum sample sizes applied in many LSA, where the minimum sample size is often set to 150 schools, with one class per school. This rule is based on the precision requirement for the main outcome of these studies, which is usually a scale score with an overall mean of 500 and a standard deviation of 100. The sampling error of this score should be below 5 (the coefficient of variation would consequently be below 1%). If we assume a typical ICC of 0.3 and a medium class size of 25, and data originating from complex samples (requiring weights to be applied), the required sample size at Level 2 would indeed be approximately 150. This outcome explains why the sample size in some countries needs to be increased when, for example, the countries have larger ICCs or smaller classes.

In Models 3 and 4, the covariance distribution had an effect on the coefficient of variation of γ_{00}. For comparable ICC levels, the coefficient of variation was smaller in the case where the covariance was stronger between rather than within clusters. The behavior of the coefficient of variation of the parameter of interest was uniform for these two models. Figure 5.3 displays the respective curves.

Because the effect of weights in Models 3 and 4 was similar to the effect in Models 1 and 2, we decided not to display the effect graphically. The graph represents results for unweighted data. Equations fitted to the curves (separated for weighted/unweighted data) are presented in Appendix Tables A6 and A7, which are accompanied by additional graphs. The shape of the curves looks identical to the shape presented in the preceding figure. The scale, however, has shifted. The coefficient of variation has become—for the comparable settings—slightly smaller in Models 3 and 4, meaning that the estimates of the mean of random intercepts became slightly more precise, especially when an explanatory variable was added at Level 2.

---

44 For Model 1, this is due to the design of the model: no explanatory variable is included.

5.1.3 Variance of random intercepts

The variance of the random intercepts (parameter U_0) represents the proportion of the total variance attributed to the between-group level. Figure 5.4 displays the relationship between the explored sample settings and the coefficient of variation of the targeted parameter for the empty model (Model 1). The interrelations again followed quadratic courses. The respective equations can be obtained from Appendix Tables A8 and A9.

Figure 5.4: CV (%) of the variance of random intercepts by weight status, ICC, and sample size at both levels: Model 1

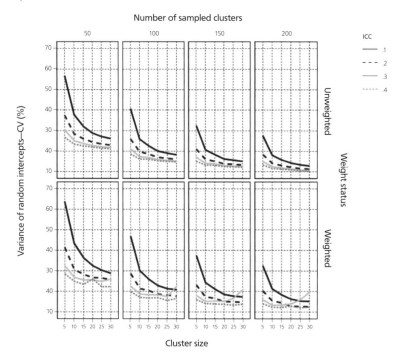

The coefficient of variation of the variance of random intercepts is clearly much larger here than it was for the model parameters discussed in the previous sections. Across all explored settings, the coefficient ranged from 10% up to 93%, with an average of 22%. This finding is in agreement with Afshartous's (1995) findings because it indicates the need to have significantly larger sample sizes when the main focus of interest is estimation of variance components rather than of fixed effects.

The effect of the ICC on the coefficient of variation of this parameter is inverted compared to the effect on the coefficient of variation of γ_{00}. The lower the ICC, the higher the coefficient of variation of the variance of random intercepts. This pattern means that this parameter can be measured more precisely when the ICC is higher, an outcome that is intuitively understood. Because the total variance was fixed,[45] the

---

45 The total variance was fixed to 10,000 (refer to Section 4.1).

parameter itself increased with increasing ICC levels, making it "easier" to measure it precisely (refer to Section 5.2.2 for further discussion).

The use of weights again increased the coefficient of variation of this parameter by, on average, a factor of approximately 1.1.

Note that the change in the coefficient of variation of the considered parameter seems to be notably large when stepping from 5 to 10 units sampled per cluster, especially for low ICCs. In fact, the gain in precision is not so much larger when, for example, doubling sample sizes at Level 1 than when doubling sample sizes at Level 2. This finding might also be of particular interest with respect to cost considerations.

Finally, we can see from Figure 5.4 that the estimates become a little unstable for weighted data when the within-cluster sample sizes are large.

When we look at the results for the other models, it is apparent that the curves are the same shape as in Model 1 but that they have shifted on the scale: the coefficients of variation have increased slightly with the increasing complexity of the model (refer to Figures 5.5 and 5.6). This is especially true for low ICCs. Introducing an explanatory variable at Level 2 has thus made it harder to estimate, with high precision, the variance of the random intercept. The effect of weights is similar to Model 1, so we again elected not to display this effect graphically but to compare the models in illustrative ways instead.

Figure 5.5: CV (%) of the variance of random intercepts by ICC, model, and sample size at both levels: Covariance Distribution Case 1 (20 at within and 10 at between level), unweighted data

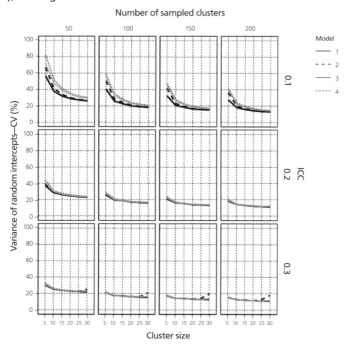

Figure 5.6: CV (%) of the variance of intercepts by ICC, model, and sample size at both levels: Covariance Distribution Case 2 (10 at within and 20 at between level), unweighted data

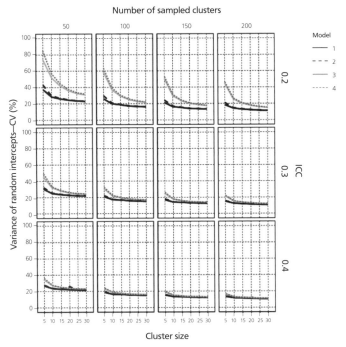

Figures 5.5 and 5.6 show the results of our analysis of unweighted data. The considered cases of covariance distributions have a barely noticeable effect for Model 2 but become significant in Models 3 and 4. For example, the explored coefficient of variation is approximately twice as large for ICC = 0.2 and small cluster sizes in the case where the covariance is stronger between than within groups. In general, differences in the coefficients of variation of the variance of random intercepts between the different models and between the different ICC levels become marginal for increasing sample sizes at both levels.

Tables A8 to A15 of the appendix give the quadratic equations separately for all different models and sample scenarios. Each of these tables is accompanied by figures that give diagrammatic form to the tables' contents.

5.1.4 Fixed slope

The parameter β_1 in Models 2 and 3 indicates the association between the dependent and explanatory variables. In our example, the parameter is an estimate of the simulated relationship between SES and achievement at the individual level. In Models 2 and 3, this slope is "fixed"—the relationship is assumed to be the same in each cluster, or school.

Figure 5.7 displays how precisely this parameter can be measured under varying population and sample conditions. As we expected, the coefficient of variation again decreased with increasing sample sizes. The covariance distribution also played an important role: when the covariance between SES and the achievement variable was stronger between than within groups (covariance is 10 within and 20 between groups), the coefficient of variation of the fixed slope was approximately double in all sampling settings. Note that the influence of the ICC on the coefficient of variation of this parameter, although present, was negligible and so is not considered in the graphs.

The effect of weights on the coefficient of variation of this model parameter was no different from what it was for all other explored coefficients of variation: all increased by roughly a factor of 1.1. Tables A16 to A19 of the appendix (with accompanying figures) present the respective quadratic equations.

Figure 5.7: CV (%) of the fixed slope by model, covariance distribution, and sample size at both levels: unweighted data

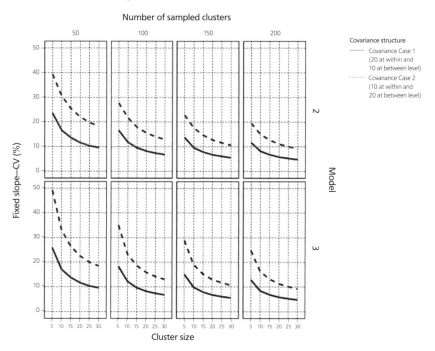

Similar to the finding for the model parameter ε (residual variance), the increase in total sample size determines the gain in precision, while the level (group or within group) on which the sample sizes are increased is of minor importance. For example, doubling the total sample from 1,000 to 2,000 individuals barely matters when the group level sample size is doubled from 100 to 200 and the within-group sample size is kept at 10, or when the number of sampled clusters is kept at 100 and the within-group sample size is doubled from 10 to 20.

5.1.5   Slope of random intercepts

The parameter γ_{01}, here referred to as the "slope of random intercepts," introduces an explanatory variable at the group level in a hierarchical model. In our example, the mean SES level in a school served as the group-level explanatory variable. In other examples, the parameter captures any contextual effects that can be measured at the group level.

Figures 5.8 and 5.9 present the association between the coefficient of variation of parameter γ_{01} and the various sample and population parameters, separated by models and the considered cases of covariance distribution.

The figures immediately make clear that it is much harder to estimate this parameter than all previously discussed parameters (under most settings) with a high degree of precision. First, we can readily see that increasing the group-level sample size (e.g., the number of schools) leads to higher precision gains than does increasing the sample size within groups (e.g., students within schools); this finding is in line with the discussed literature (Cohen, 1998; Mok, 1995; Snijders, 2005). Secondly, we can see that the covariance distribution plays a very important role. In Model 3 (Figure 5.8), the variation coefficients almost double when the covariance is stronger within groups than between groups. As a reminder, we consider two cases of the split of the covariance at the within- and the between-cluster level. In the first case, the within-level covariance was set to 20 and the between-level covariance was set to 10. The distribution over Levels 1 and 2 was reversed in the second case.

Figure 5.8: CV (%) of the slope of random intercepts by ICC, covariance distribution, and sample size at both levels: Model 3, unweighted data

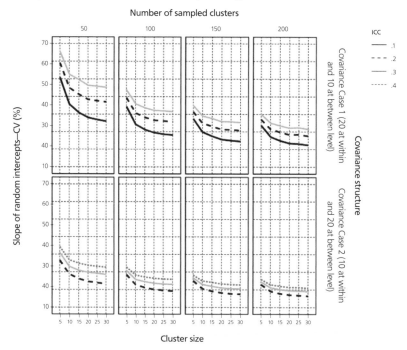

Figure 5.9: CV (%) of the slope of random intercepts by ICC, covariance distribution, and sample size at both levels: Model 4, unweighted data

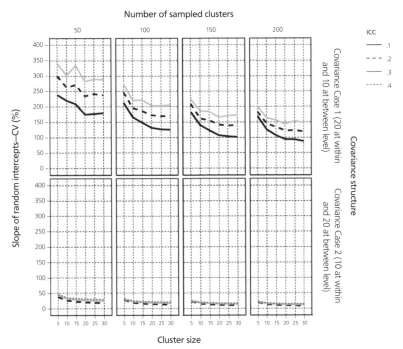

In Model 4, the differences of the coefficient of variation between the two covariance cases also reached much higher levels (up to a factor of 13), as can be seen in Figure 5.9. This result suggests that when the covariance is strong at the within-group level, the slope of random intercepts can barely be measured with sufficient confidence for models with explanatory variables at both the within- and the between-group level.

The ICC also played a significant role. With increasing ICCs, the coefficient of variation of γ_{01} also increased. Similar to observations of parameter γ_{00}, the effect became larger as cluster sample sizes increased but remained relatively stable as the numbers of sampled clusters increased.

Weights influenced the coefficient of variation of the slope of random intercepts in similar vein to the other explored parameters (increasing by a factor of approximately 1.1). Tables A20 to A23 in the appendix display the quadratic equations, listed by model, covariance distribution case, weights, ICC, and number of sampled clusters. Each table is accompanied with a graph depicting the table's contents. Note that for Model 4, the slope of the coefficients of variation for Case 1 of the covariance distribution is not as smooth as it usually is for all settings with small group-level sample sizes (upper left-hand graphs of Figure 5.9). As a consequence, the fit of the quadratic curves to the slope leads to lower R squares.

Given the extreme gradient in sampling error between the two examined cases of covariance distribution, more research involving other covariance distribution settings is required to explore the behavior of SEs.

5.1.6 Mean of random slopes

An individual-level explanatory variable can influence the outcome variable in different ways (i.e., magnitudes or even directions). This influence can be modeled by introducing a further random term into the model ($\beta_1 = \gamma_{10} + U_1$). This was the scenario considered in Model 4, where the term γ_{10} stands for the mean of the random slopes. But how precisely can we measure this term when using sample data?

Figure 5.10 provides a partial answer to this question. As the graphs suggest, the case of covariance distribution had a significant influence on the sampling error of this parameter as well. The coefficient of variation approximately doubled when the covariance between the explanatory and the outcome variable was stronger at the between-group level. With the latter case, minimum sample sizes of > 5 within clusters are indicated when the parameter itself needs to be significant (i.e., different from zero) and when few clusters (< 100) are sampled. Note also that the ICC has an influence—albeit a relatively small one—on the coefficient of variation. With increasing ICC levels, the coefficient of variation decreased slightly. When weights were used, the coefficient of variation again increased by a factor of approximately 1.1.

Figure 5.10: CV (%) of the mean of random slopes by covariance distribution, ICC, and sample size at both levels: Model 4, unweighted data

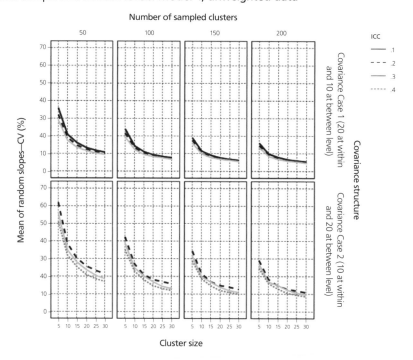

Appendix Tables A24 and A25 display the respective quadratic equations, derived separately for different covariance distribution cases, weight status, ICCs, and sample size settings.

5.1.7   Variance of random slopes

The second—and often more interesting—term in a model with random slopes is U_1, which represents the variance of the random slopes. If this term is significantly different from zero, it can be inferred that the explanatory variable is connected to the outcome variable in different magnitudes or even directions in different clusters. In our example, it could mean, for instance, that students' SES may be positively correlated to achievement in some schools but not in others.

Unfortunately, the estimation of the parameter itself seems to be affected with significant bias, which must be caused by the estimation procedure used in Mplus. As displayed in Figure 5.11, the parameter seems to depend on sample sizes even though this cannot be the case. Therefore, the obtained sampling errors also cannot be relied on either, and for this reason we have not provided graphs or equations for the coefficients of variation of this parameter.

As part of our ongoing research, we intend to conduct an in-depth exploration of the discovered parameter estimation bias.

Figure 5.11: Variance of random slopes (means over all replicates) by covariance distribution, ICC, and sample size at both levels: Model 4

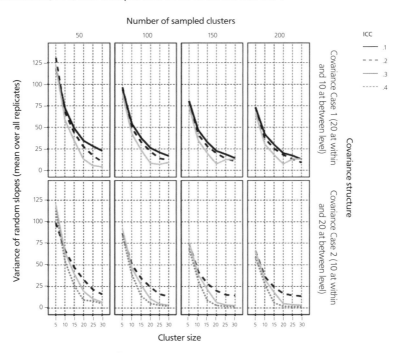

5.2 Effects of Variable Population and Sample Parameters

5.2.1 Sample sizes

As expected, the coefficients of variation of all explored parameters decreased when the sample sizes increased, regardless of whether the increase was within clusters or pertained to the number of sampled clusters (or both). The dependency between sample sizes and coefficients of variation always followed a quadratic curve progression within the explored settings. For example, increasing sample size decreased the diminishing effect on the coefficient of variation. The curves could be approximated with quadratic equations that fitted extremely well to the observed curves for most parameters (R squares mostly > 0.95). This general observation was affected neither by the intraclass correlation coefficients, the weight status, and the covariance distribution, nor by the complexity of the explored model.

The magnitude of this decrease, and whether the effect is more pronounced with sample size increases on one or the other hierarchical level, can, however, depend on all these factors and so were different for the explored model parameters. We detailed this matter in Section 5.1.

In contradiction to general rules of thumb recommended in the literature (e.g., Hox, 1995; Kreft, 1996; Mok, 1995), our findings suggest that the required sample sizes depend heavily on the parameter of interest. In particular, sample size requirements were very different if the focus of interest was the estimation of fixed model parameters or, rather, the estimation of variances. Inferences from another simulation study (Afshartous, 1995) support these findings. Also, and in agreement with the literature (Cohen, 1998; Mok, 1995; Snijders, 2005), it appears that it is more effective to increase the number of sampled clusters than the cluster sample size if the research interest concerns macro-level regression coefficients. If the focus is on variance estimates, however, the level on which the sample size is increased appears to be of less importance.

In Section 5.1, curves were displayed according to their dependency on the cluster size. It is possible, of course, to look at the interrelations between parameter precision and sample sizes from different perspectives. Figures 5.12 and 5.13 illustrate this concept. They show, for one of the explored parameters, how the curves would look if the total sample sizes or the number of sampled clusters respectively were set as the explanatory variable. Interested readers can utilize the appendix equations to produce such graphs for other parameters themselves.

Although the following matters are not part of the main scope of this paper, we encourage readers to keep two related issues in mind when determining required sample sizes:

1. Currently, available estimation methods can produce biased parameter estimates if the sample size (at either level) is small. The literature provides a variety of articles on this topic (refer to, for example, Asparouhov et al., 2006; Bell et al., 2010; Graubard & Korn, 1996; Korn & Graubard, 2003; Kovacevic & Rai, 2003; Rabe-Hesketh & Skrondal, 2006). Simulation studies, however, indicate that as

Figure 5.12: CV (%) of the fixed slope by covariance distribution, ICC, and total sample size, averaged over Models 2 and 3 and weight status

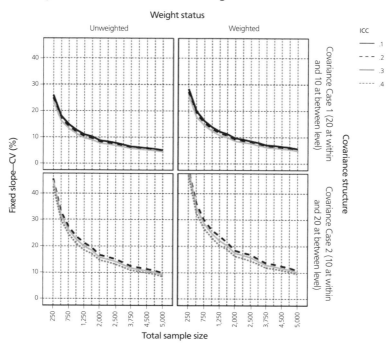

the number of clusters and the cluster sample size increase, the parameter bias is generally eliminated. Estimation methods that possess this property are referred to as approximately unbiased. All currently available software packages that accommodate hierarchical modeling apply such estimation methods. The degree of parameter bias depends on the model itself, the model parameter of interest, and the sample conditions. As a result of data collected as a side product of this study, we do not recommend dropping below a within-cluster sample size of 10 because doing so risks biasing the parameter estimation.

2. The estimation of the sampling errors can be biased. For the explored parameters and conditions, our results suggest that the bias can be substantial[46] if the number of sampled clusters is below 100. Further details on this topic can be found in Section 4.4.1.

---

46 Depending on the parameter of interest, the SE was overestimated by up to a factor of 4.

Figure 5.13: CV (%) of the fixed slope by covariance distribution, ICC, and sample size at both levels, averaged over Models 2 and 3 and weight status

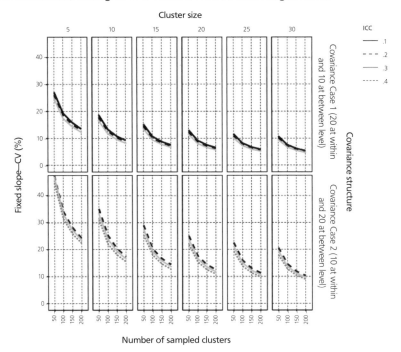

5.2.2   Intraclass correlation coefficients

The intraclass correlation coefficient (ICC) had no influence on the coefficient of variation of the residual variance (parameter ε). The coefficients of variation of the parameters γ_{00} (mean of random intercepts) and γ_{01} (slope of random intercepts) grew with increasing ICC levels. Preliminary findings suggest that the same association was in effect for the coefficient of variation of the variance of random slopes (parameter U_1). For the former parameters, the effect of ICC diminished as sample sizes within clusters increased.

When we explored the impact of the ICC on the coefficients of variation of the remaining parameters—U_0, variance of random intercepts; γ_{10}, mean of random slopes, and β_1, fixed slope—we found the inverse effect: as the ICC levels increased, the coefficients of variation decreased. The effect for the latter parameter was, however, minimal.

We ask readers, when considering these results, to keep the design of this study in mind. In general, variance and regression coefficients are easier to measure precisely if they are bigger, while within- and across-cluster means are harder to measure precisely when the variance is higher. This pattern can easily be seen when looking at extreme cases. If the variance is 0 at any level, then all the individuals or all the clusters are alike and any sample will estimate the true mean correctly. If, however, the variance is very big, the estimates of the mean can be very different from one sample to another and, even though unbiased, can be very imprecise (high sampling error).

This pattern holds true for both levels—individuals and clusters. The regression coefficients link to the variances and covariances as follows:[47]

$$regression\ coefficient = \frac{cov(achievement,\ ses)}{variance(achievement)}$$

The pattern is also valid at both levels: smaller regression coefficients are harder to measure with high precision. Because the overall variance in our simulation study was fixed, a higher ICC caused greater variance between clusters, leaving U_0 measured more precisely and the mean γ_{00} less precisely. Also, because the covariance is fixed for each case of the covariance distribution, larger ICCs and higher variance between clusters induce smaller regression coefficients for the random slopes γ_{01} along with higher coefficients of variation of γ_{01}. However, larger ICCs also mean lower variance within clusters, which leads to higher regression coefficients β_1 and lower coefficients of variation.

Our efforts to compare these findings with earlier research proved fairly unproductive. Although a few authors have explored the effect of ICC on bias in HLM parameter estimation (Asparouhov et al., 2006; Kovacevic & Rai, 2003) and bias in the estimation of sampling errors (Maas & Hox, 2005), we could not find explicit statements about the influence of ICC on the sampling errors of different parameters in hierarchical models.

5.2.3 Covariance distributions

During this research, we explored only two cases of covariance distribution. As such, we could not make general inferences about the gradual effects of varying covariance distributions. Comparisons could only be made between the two considered cases.

The covariance distribution had no effect on the coefficients of variation of any of the explored parameters in Models 1 and 2, except for the fixed slope. For Model 1, this was caused by the design of the model (no explanatory variable was introduced). Also, no effect was observed on parameter ε in any model.

The first considered case of covariance distribution (20 at within-group and 10 at between-group level) was connected to higher coefficients of variation compared to the second considered case (10 at within-group and 20 at between-group level) for the parameters γ_{00} and γ_{01}. For the latter parameter, the differences in the coefficients of variation were extreme, particularly when explanatory variables on both levels were introduced to the model (Model 4; refer to section 5.1.5).

---

47 This formula refers to simple OLS estimation. Note that different procedures (maximum likelihood estimation) are used to estimate coefficients in HLM.

On examining the effect on the coefficients of variation of the parameters U_0, β_1, and γ_{10}, we found that the ratios were higher when the covariance distribution was stronger between groups (Covariance Case 2). We emphasize, though, that the effect of the covariance distribution on the coefficients of variation of the parameters β_1, and particularly γ_{01}, was even more pronounced than the effect of varying sample sizes.

In the simulation studies conducted so far (refer to Section 2.3), the covariance distribution was always fixed. For this reason, the results cannot be compared to previous related research.

5.2.4   Weights

The weights applied in this research increased the coefficients of variation of all explored parameters consistently by a factor of approximately 1.1. But concluding that not using weights is preferable because this practice increases the sampling error would be a serious mistake: using sampling weights is the only way to prevent bias when estimating parameters from data collected with a complex sample design.

The method used to simulate the weights should be kept in mind when evaluating this result (refer to Section 4.2.4). Preliminary evaluations of the findings with real data[48] showed that the aforementioned factor only held true if the actual Level 2 weights followed a Poisson distribution. This is what happens when the implemented sample design fulfills the following conditions:

1. The clusters (e.g., schools) are selected with probabilities proportional to their size;

2. The sizes of the schools in the respective country are close to a Poisson distribution; and

3. No oversampling is performed in any explicit stratum.

If these conditions are not fulfilled or, in other words, the Level 2 weights deviate from a Poisson distribution, the weights may have larger (or sometimes smaller) effects on the coefficients of variation of the different model parameters.

These conditions are reasonably standard assumptions for the presented research because they apply to many LSA. However, the sample designs for (e.g.) particular countries frequently deviate from this ideal condition for many reasons. It is well known that, in most instances, sampling weights increase the sampling error and hence the coefficients of variation. The effect could, however, depend on the distribution of these weights and maybe even their correlation with the dependent variable. Further research is needed to give a more exact understanding of the effect of weights and thereby avoid making assumptions about their distribution.

---

48 Informal evaluations of the findings were conducted with data from the TIMSS 2007 Grade 8 population. Nine countries were examined.

We were unable to identify a single article in the literature focusing on the effects of weights in HLM on the sampling variance of the estimates. However, in reference to a side product of their research, Grilli and Pratesi (2004) and Pfeffermann et al. (1998) point out that using weights increases the sampling variance and provides less biased parameter estimates. When we compared the data presented in the tables in Grilli and Pratesi's article with the findings of our research, we found similar degrees of sampling variance. We also found when scouring the literature with respect to the debate on the role of sampling weights in multilevel models that Zaccarin and Donati (2008) agreed that weights have relevant effects on parameter estimates and their sampling errors. However, the two authors did not investigate the subject in more detail.

5.2.5   Model complexity

The four models considered in this research were built with increasing complexity.[49] This complexity influenced the coefficients of variation of all observed parameters except one. The influence varied, however, with the parameter of interest as well as with the considered case of covariance distribution.

Model complexity did not appear to influence the coefficient of variation of parameter ε (residual variance).

As was demonstrated in Section 5.1.2, the coefficients of variation of parameter γ_{00} (mean of random intercepts) behaved uniformly for Models 1 and 2, and also for Models 3 and 4. However, the coefficient of variation was smaller for the latter two models than for the simpler Models 1 and 2. We can infer, therefore, that the introduction of the Level 2 explanatory variable induces a gain in the precision of the estimation of parameter γ_{00}. This effect was more pronounced when the covariance was stronger between clusters (see Figure 5.14), a finding that aligns with observations made by Raudenbush (1997), who proposed using covariates in order to determine the optimal design of cluster randomized trials.

If we look at parameter U_0 (variance of random intercepts), we can see that the effect of the model complexity is inverted. The model's coefficient of variation has increased as the model has become more complex. The differences are marginal, however, as long as the covariance is strong at the within-cluster level, but when the covariance strengthens between groups, Models 1 and 2 show significantly smaller coefficients of variation than do Models 3 and 4 for the discussed parameter. The effect decreases with increasing ICC levels (refer to Figure 5.15).

---

49 Note that even the most complex model explored in this research is still a relatively simple one.

Figure 5.14: CV (%) of the mean of random intercepts by ICC, model, and cluster size: average over weight status and numbers of sampled clusters

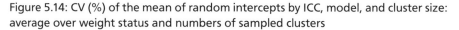
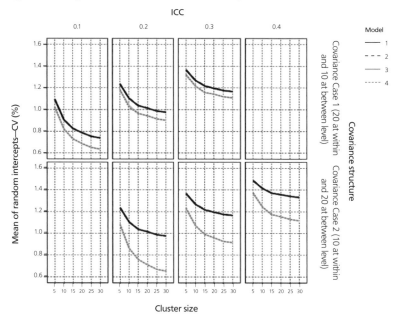

Figure 5.15: CV (%) of the variance of random intercepts by ICC, model, and cluster size: average over weight status and numbers of sampled clusters

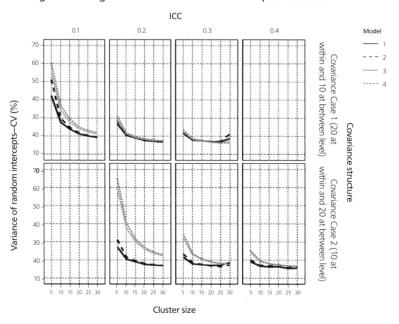

A look at the coefficients of variation of model parameter β_1 (fixed slope, explored in Models 2 and 3) reveals very little difference between the two models when the covariance is strong at the within-cluster level, as illustrated in Figure 5.16. For the other considered covariance case, however, the parameter is estimated with less precision in Model 3, especially when the within-cluster sample size is small.

Finally, we found that the coefficient of variation of the slope of random intercepts (parameter γ_{01}) also increased with model complexity (it was higher in Model 4 than in Model 3). This finding held true for both covariance cases. However, as illustrated in Figure 5.17, the effect became much more pronounced when the covariance was stronger within clusters (the coefficient of variation increased by up to factor 6).

Figure 5.16: CV (%) of the fixed slope by ICC, model, and cluster size: average over weight status and numbers of sampled clusters

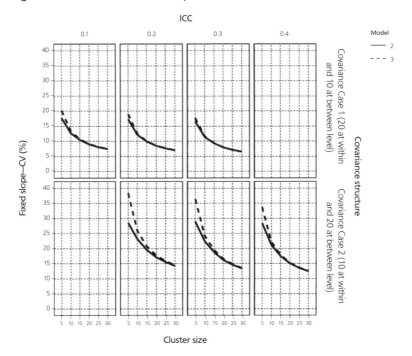

Figure 5.17: CV (%) of the slope of random intercepts by ICC, model, and cluster size: average over weight status and numbers of sampled clusters

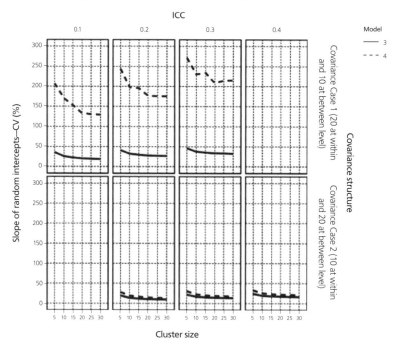

5.3 Practical Use of Outcome Equations

Our intention in conducting this research was to provide outcomes that would be of practical use for researchers wanting to determine required sample sizes for a particular research project during its planning phase. We also anticipated that these outcomes would enable researchers doing secondary analysis of available LSA datasets to evaluate, in advance, the precision range that they could expect from the available data, depending on their research questions.

The graphs presented throughout Sections 5.1 and 5.2 above and the graphs accompanying the appendix tables offer a good starting point when determining required sample sizes under specific conditions. Ranges of sampling errors of specific model parameters to be expected for varying sample and population conditions can be easily read off these graphs. They also allow users unable to exactly specify population parameters, such as ICC or covariance distributions, in advance to draw conclusions relating to possible variations of sampling error.

The appendix contains the estimated quadratic equations for all sample and population conditions explored throughout this publication. Note that although some of the approximated quadratic equations appear to be insignificant, they still have very high R^2 values. This is the case, for example, for the equations describing the relationships between sample sizes and the coefficients of variation of the variance of the random intercepts (Appendix Tables A8 to A15), and it is due to the fact that very few numerical values were used to build the curves (four or six respectively in this case). In fact, each of these numerical values represents an average of 6,000 replicates and therefore has a high reliability in its own right. This means that if the model goodness of fit is high, the equations are very reliable, even when their p values are not below 0.05.

In the remainder of this chapter, we use two examples to explain how the appendix equations can be of practical use. We emphasize, though, that the results are only valid under the specified model assumptions and cannot be generalized to different sample and population conditions (refer also to Section 6). For example, it is not certain whether the equations will hold for, say, within-cluster sample sizes of 50, or for different ranges or distributions of covariances. In particular, caution is advised for all model parameters where the coefficient of variation depends heavily on the covariance distribution. More research is required to explore the degree to which we can generalize the results to other settings and conditions.

In order to make use of the outcome equations in the appendix, the following steps need to be performed:

1. Formulate research question;

2. Specify the hierarchical model and the parameter of interest;

3. Determine fixed population and sample parameters;

4. Choose, apply, and solve equation;

5. Discuss limitations of observed result(s)

Example 1

A researcher is interested in reporting levels of association between family SES and academic achievement for various education systems. Model 2 is the appropriate model to use when endeavoring to answer the research question. The parameter of interest is β_1 (fixed slope). The researcher determines the parameter as being sufficiently precise if the SE takes no more than 10% of its value. For instance, if the estimate of β_1 is 18, its sampling error must be below 1.8. (Note that such a requirement can also be driven by the request to identify relevant differences between education systems within certain significance levels; see also Example 2 in this regard.)

The first step requires specification of each education system's sample and population conditions. (For the sake of simplicity, we use only one education system when describing the steps to be conducted.)

Let's assume the researcher wants to test one class per school; the average class size is 25. From previous research, it is known that the covariance between SES and achievement is stronger within than between groups and that the ICC is 0.3. The sample of schools will be selected with probabilities proportional to the size of the schools, which means that the researchers will need to apply weights when they later carry out their analyses.

So, how many schools need to be sampled in order to answer the research question with the specified confidence levels? The correct equation can be found in Table A17 of the appendix, an excerpt from which is given here as Figure 5.18.

Figure 5.18: Excerpt from Appendix Table 17

Case	ICC	Cluster size	Unweighted					Weighted				
			Model summary		Parameter estimates			Model summary		Parameter estimates		
			R square	Sig.	Constant	b1	b2	R square	Sig.	Constant	b1	b2
Covariance Case 1 (20 at within and 10 at between level)	.1	5	.993	.084	33.1	-.206	5.08E-04	.995	.068	36.2	-.222	5.35E-04
		10	.997	.055	23.7	-.146	3.54E-04	.997	.056	26.1	-.161	3.91E-04
		15	.995	.073	19.8	-.126	3.18E-04	.995	.067	21.6	-.136	3.36E-04
		20	.996	.067	16.8	-.106	2.63E-04	.995	.069	18.5	-.115	2.86E-04
		25	.995	.069	14.9	-.092	2.26E-04	.994	.076	16.7	-.107	2.75E-04
		30	.995	.068	14.0	-.088	2.20E-04	.995	.072	15.3	-.096	2.38E-04
	.2	5	.993	.083	32.6	-.204	5.03E-04	.994	.076	35.3	-.216	5.25E-04
		10	.997	.055	22.7	-.140	3.39E-04	.997	.058	24.9	-.151	3.61E-04
		15	.995	.073	18.8	-.120	3.02E-04	.995	.072	20.7	-.132	3.30E-04
		20	.996	.067	15.9	-.100	2.49E-04	.996	.066	17.6	-.110	2.74E-04
		25	.995	.068	14.1	-.086	2.13E-04	.996	.064	15.9	-.100	2.48E-04
		30	.995	.069	13.2	-.083	2.08E-04	.996	.066	14.6	-.093	2.32E-04
	.3	5	.993	.083	31.2	-.195	4.81E-04	.995	.069	34.3	-.218	5.46E-04
		10	.997	.055	21.3	-.132	3.19E-04	.996	.062	23.3	-.144	3.54E-04
		15	.995	.073	17.6	-.112	2.82E-04	.995	.072	19.7	-.128	3.27E-04
		20	.996	.066	14.9	-.093	2.31E-04	.996	.062	16.6	-.105	2.64E-04
		25	.995	.068	13.1	-.080	1.98E-04	.997	.059	14.5	-.089	2.20E-04
		30	.995	.069	12.3	-.078	1.94E-04	.996	.067	13.6	-.086	2.16E-04
			.994	.077	53.6	-.33.6				58.0	-.355	8.65E-04

When the numbers are inserted into equation (6),

$$y = b_0 + b_1 z + b_2 z^2$$

becomes

$$10 = 14.5 - .089 z + 2.2E^{-4}z^2,$$

with z being the number of clusters to be sampled. Solving the equation for z by applying the binomial theorem[50] leads to two results (rounded):

$$z = \{345; 59\}$$

Because the formula is only valid in a range from 50 to 200 clusters, the larger value, 345, should be dismissed. Therefore, 59 would be the estimated appropriate Level 2 sample size for that education system.

---

50 For convenience, users can refer to various programs, available on the internet, that solve quadratic equations (e.g., http://www.math.com/students/calculators/source/quadratic.htm).

When determining the expected coefficient of variation (in this example, 10%), the researcher would need to consider the valid ranges of this ratio under the given sample and population conditions. If he considers the values outside the valid range, the equation is either not solvable or the solution(s) of the equation take(s) values outside the explored ranges. If, for instance, a value of 5% rather than 10% is considered, the equation cannot be solved. The graphics in the results sections of this section of the monograph provide good reference points for valid ranges of coefficients of variation.

Example 2

A researcher is interested in comparing levels of association between family SES and academic achievement for two countries. Because she first wants to determine if a dataset originating from an LSA survey has data that will allow her to answer her research question, she needs to know how precisely the parameter was measured in that survey.

Again, Model 2 is the appropriate model to be applied and β_1 is the relevant parameter. Let's assume that both education systems fulfill the same preconditions as in Example 1. Let's also assume that a sample of 150 schools has been selected in both countries. The researcher can apply the same equation as the one in the previous example, but this time the sampled number of schools would need to be inserted:

$y = 14.5 - .089 \times 150 + 2.2E^{-4} \times 150^2$

$y = 6.1\%$.

The researcher can thus expect the 95% confidence interval of the parameter β_1 to be roughly within ± 12% of β_1), which implies that she will be able to identify, with respect to this parameter, only rather large differences between countries as significant under the given sample and population conditions.

Note that many further considerations other than those discussed above and in Section 5.2.1 drive the decision on sample sizes. For example, expected non-response rates, booklet rotation schemes, research interest in subgroups, and the like also need to be considered. However, these aspects are beyond the scope of this research and so are not addressed here.

6. Limitations and Need for Further Research

As is the case with any research, readers need to consider the presented results within the context of limitations. Also, the process of posing and answering particular research questions typically generates more questions that need to be explored through further research.

Most importantly with respect to the current research, readers need to remember that we considered only clearly determined population and sampling settings; reference to other settings may have produced different results. The extent to which our findings can be generalized certainly requires further investigation. The graduated influence of varying covariance distributions should be of particular ongoing interest given that this feature had large influences on the coefficients of variation of the various model parameters. Also, it may be worth exploring the influence of higher values of intraclass correlation coefficients because ICCs above 0.4 can be obtained for students in highly selective education systems.

We checked the results emerging from the simulations for their applicability to real data. We did this in preliminary format, using a small sample of real datasets from TIMSS 2007 (Grade 8 population). However, a systematic evaluation would be desirable in order to demonstrate the degree of applicability to real survey data.

Our preliminary verifications showed one limitation of this research: if the sample selection probabilities at Level 2 deviate from the explored conditions, the presented equations can no longer be applied (see Section 5.2.4 for more details). This phenomenon occurs in LSA when oversampling within certain explicit sampling strata is employed in order to accommodate precise parameter estimation for subgroups. Further research is needed to shed more light on this occurrence.

Extended investigations may also show whether the results hold true for distributions of the dependent and explanatory variables other than the ones explored here.

Finally, more research needs to be carried out on more complex models. A particular focus on random coefficients appears to be desirable.

7. Summary and Conclusions

The purpose of this study was to explore the associations between sample sizes at different levels of clustered data and the sampling precision of the results derived from hierarchical linear models (HLM). As outcomes, we provided graphs and equation tables that show the connection between the two concepts.

Our research was strictly oriented toward the needs of researchers wanting to apply HLM analyses to data collected in large-scale educational surveys (LSA), or survey designers with similar interests. We considered the specifics of such datasets and used a Monte Carlo simulation study in order to explore various population and sample conditions. In particular, the explored settings varied in terms of the following:

- Sample sizes of and within clusters;
- Intraclass correlation coefficients;
- Covariance distribution; and
- Weight status.

We explored, for all settings, four different hierarchical linear models with increasing complexity. We used the coefficient of variation, displayed as a percentage, to measure sampling precision.

On average, over all explored settings and models, the parameters γ_{00} (mean of random intercepts) and ε (residual variance) could be measured with the highest sampling precision levels. On the contrary, the parameter γ_{01} (slope of random intercepts) was the parameter that was measured with the poorest precision. This was particularly the case when the covariance distribution between the outcome and the explanatory variable was stronger at the within-cluster level.

As we expected, the coefficients of variation of all explored parameters decreased when sample size increased. The dependency between sample size and coefficient of variation could always be described by a quadratic curve progression, within the explored setting, such that increasing sample size decreased the diminishing effect on the coefficient of variation. This general observation was affected neither by the intraclass correlation coefficients, the weight status, or the covariance distribution, nor by the complexity of the explored model. The magnitude of this decrease, and whether the effect was more pronounced with sample size increases on one or the other hierarchical level, could depend, however, on all these factors and was different for the explored model parameters.

In conclusion, the results showed that the required sample sizes depended heavily on the parameter of interest. In particular, sample size requirements differed widely for the estimation of fixed-model parameters and the estimation of variances. In agreement with the literature, it appears that increasing the number of sampled clusters rather than the cluster sample size is more effective if the research interest concerns macro-level regression coefficients. If the focus is on variance estimates, however, the level on which the sample size is increased appears to be of less importance.

It is worthwhile noting that the reduction in the coefficient of variation of the variance of random intercepts (parameter U_0) seemed to become notably larger as we stepped from 5 to 10 sampled units per cluster, especially for low ICCs. In fact, the gain in precision was not that much larger when, for example, doubling sample sizes at Level 1 than when doubling sample sizes at Level 2. This finding could have particular relevance with respect to cost considerations.

The intraclass correlation coefficient had no influence on the coefficient of variation of the residual variance, while the coefficients of variation of the parameters γ_{00} (mean of random intercepts) and γ_{01} (slope of random intercepts) increased with larger ICC values. This effect diminished with larger within-cluster sample sizes. Exploring the impact of the ICC on the coefficients of variation of the remaining considered parameters—U_0 (variance of random intercepts), γ_{10} (mean of random slopes), and γ_1 (fixed slope)—produced the inverse effect: a decrease in the coefficients of variation as the ICC levels increased.

As a new contribution to this research area, we considered two cases of covariance distribution. We found that the effect of the covariance distribution on the coefficients of variation of the parameters β_1 (fixed slope) and particularly γ_{01} (slope of random intercepts) was—at least within the limitations/conditions of this research—even more pronounced than the effect of varying sample sizes. We noted no effect on the coefficients of variation of any explored parameter, other than the fixed slope, in Models 1 and 2. We also observed no effect on parameter ε in any model.

Compared to the second considered case of covariance distribution (10 at within-group and 20 at between-group level) for the parameters γ_{00} and γ_{01}, the first considered case of covariance distribution (20 at within-group and 10 at between-group level) was connected to higher coefficients of variation. The differences in the coefficients of variation were extreme for parameter γ_{01}, particularly when explanatory variables on both levels were introduced to the model. For the parameters U_0, β_1, and γ_{10}, the coefficients of variation were higher if the covariance distribution was 20 between groups and 10 within, rather than the other way around.

Weights, which have to be applied to allow unbiased estimates in LSA, enlarged the coefficients of variation of all explored parameters consistently by a factor of approximately 1.1. Preliminary evaluations of the findings with real data showed that this factor held true only if the actual Level 2 weights followed a Poisson distribution. This was the case if the implemented sample design fulfilled particular conditions, detailed in the respective chapter.

Model complexity had an influence on the coefficients of variation of all observed parameters except for the residual variance. The influence varied with the parameter of interest as well as with the considered case of covariance distribution. The coefficients of variation of parameter γ_{00} were smaller in the models that included a macro-level explanatory variable. The effect was more pronounced in the case where the covariance was stronger between clusters.

For parameters U_0 and β_1, however, the precision diminished with increasing model complexity, but the differences remained marginal as long as the covariance was strong at the within-cluster level. For these two parameters, the effect decreased with increasing ICC levels. The coefficient of variation of parameter γ_{01} also increased with model complexity, but the effect here was clearly more pronounced when the covariance was stronger within clusters.

We end by emphasizing that all findings can be deemed valid only within the explored ranges of sampling and population settings. The degree of generalizability of the results to other settings and conditions will be the subject of further research.

APPENDIX

Table A1: Overview of sampling scenarios explored

All sampling scenarios presented in the following table were analyzed (i) without the application of sampling weights, and (ii) with the application of sampling weights, which gives 288 explored scenarios in total.

Scenario number	Covariance structure	ICC	Number of sampled clusters	Cluster size
1		0.1	50	5
2	Covariance Case 1 (20 at within and			10
3	10 at between level)			15
4				20
5				25
6				30
7			100	5
8				10
9				15
10				20
11				25
12				30
13			150	5
14				10
15				15
16				20
17				25
18				30
19			200	5
20				10
21				15
22				20
23				25
24				30
25		0.2	50	5
26				10
27				15
28				20
29				25
30				30
31			100	5
32				10
33				15
34				20
35				25
36				30
37			150	5
38				10
39				15
40				20
41				25
42				30
43			200	5
44				10
45				15
46				20
47				25
48				30
49		0.3	50	5
50				10
51				15
52				20
53				25
54				30
55			100	5
56				10
57				15
58				20
59				25
60				30
61			150	5
62				10
63				15
64				20
65				25
66				30
67			200	5
68				10
69				15
70				20
71				25
72				30

Table A1: Overview sampling scenarios explored (contd.)

Scenario number	Covariance structure	ICC	Number of sampled clusters	Cluster size
73		0.2	50	5
74	Covariance Case 2 (10 at within and			10
75	20 at between level)			15
76				20
77				25
78				30
79			100	5
80				10
81				15
82				20
83				25
84				30
85			150	5
86				10
87				15
88				20
89				25
90				30
91			200	5
92				10
93				15
94				20
95				25
96				30
97		0.3	50	5
98				10
99				15
100				20
101				25
102				30
103			100	5
104				10
105				15
106				20
107				25
108				30
109			150	5
110				10
111				15
112				20
113				25
114				30
115			200	5
116				10
117				15
118				20
119				25
120				30
121		0.4	50	5
122				10
123				15
124				20
125				25
126				30
127			100	5
128				10
129				15
130				20
131				25
132				30
133			150	5
134				10
135				15
136				20
137				25
138				30
139			200	5
140				10
141				15
142				20
143				25
144				30

Table A2: Results of curve estimation for the CV (%) of the residual variance: quadratic equations (model summary and parameter estimates, average over all models and both covariance cases; the independent variable is cluster size)

Number of sampled clusters	Weight status									
	Unweighted					Weighted				
	Model summary		Parameter estimates			Model summary		Parameter estimates		
	R square	Sig.	Constant	b1	b2	R square	Sig.	Constant	b1	b2
50	.969	.000	12.56	-0.660	1.25E-02	.970	.000	13.90	-0.734	1.39E-02
100	.974	.000	9.06	-0.490	9.39E-03	.975	.000	9.95	-0.534	1.02E-02
150	.975	.000	7.35	-0.396	7.59E-03	.975	.000	8.11	-0.435	8.35E-03
200	.974	.000	6.46	-0.354	6.87E-03	.976	.000	7.13	-0.389	7.51E-03

Figure A1: CV (%) of the residual variance: average over all models and both covariance cases (graphical representation of Table A2)

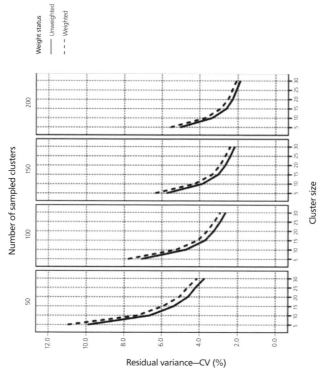

Table A3: Results of curve estimation for the CV (%) of the residual variance: quadratic equations (model summary and parameter estimates, average over all models and both covariance cases; the independent variable is number of sampled clusters)

Cluster size	Weight status										
	Unweighted					Weighted					
	Model summary		Parameter estimates			Model summary		Parameter estimates			
	R square	Sig.	Constant	b1	b2	R square	Sig.	Constant	b1	b2	
5	.989	.000	13.58	-0.085	2.11E-04	.994	.000	15.06	-0.095	2.38E-04	
10	.996	.000	9.07	-0.056	1.39E-04	.994	.000	9.93	-0.061	1.49E-04	
15	.994	.000	7.46	-0.049	1.23E-04	.994	.000	8.29	-0.055	1.40E-04	
20	.995	.000	6.33	-0.040	9.83E-05	.995	.000	6.91	-0.043	1.04E-04	
25	.994	.000	5.86	-0.039	9.88E-05	.993	.000	6.42	-0.041	1.05E-04	
30	.995	.000	5.13	-0.032	8.13E-05	.995	.000	5.66	-0.036	8.93E-05	

Figure A2: CV (%) of the residual variance: average over all models and both covariance cases (graphical representation of Table A3)

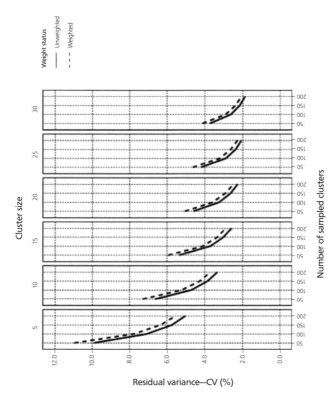

Table A4: Results of curve estimation for the CV (%) of the mean of random intercepts: quadratic equations (model summary and parameter estimates; average over Models 1 and 2 and both covariance cases; the independent variable is cluster size)

ICC	Number of sampled clusters	Weight status										
		Unweighted					Weighted					
		Model summary		Parameter estimates			Model summary		Parameter estimates			
		R square	Sig.	Constant	b1	b2	R square	Sig.	Constant	b1	b2
.1	50	.980	.000	1.71	-0.054	1.03E-03	.981	.000	1.90	-0.060	1.15E-03
	100	.984	.000	1.21	-0.038	7.23E-04	.973	.000	1.34	-0.043	8.19E-04
	150	.967	.000	0.99	-0.031	5.94E-04	.971	.000	1.09	-0.033	6.34E-04
	200	.978	.000	0.85	-0.026	4.79E-04	.975	.000	0.95	-0.030	5.76E-04
.2	50	.980	.000	1.85	-0.040	7.73E-04	.979	.000	2.02	-0.041	7.72E-04
	100	.988	.000	1.31	-0.028	5.23E-04	.989	.000	1.46	-0.032	6.09E-04
	150	.963	.000	1.07	-0.023	4.41E-04	.958	.000	1.19	-0.027	5.52E-04
	200	.982	.000	0.92	-0.018	3.30E-04	.986	.000	1.01	-0.021	3.71E-04
.3	50	.981	.000	1.99	-0.031	5.91E-04	.988	.000	2.19	-0.034	6.72E-04
	100	.993	.000	1.41	-0.021	3.81E-04	.979	.000	1.56	-0.023	4.39E-04
	150	.956	.000	1.15	-0.017	3.31E-04	.968	.000	1.27	-0.018	3.15E-04
	200	.985	.000	0.99	-0.013	2.24E-04	.975	.000	1.10	-0.016	2.95E-04
.4	50	.982	.000	2.13	-0.024	4.51E-04	.966	.000	2.33	-0.023	4.41E-04
	100	.996	.000	1.50	-0.015	2.68E-04	.981	.000	1.66	-0.017	3.15E-04
	150	.940	.000	1.23	-0.013	2.46E-04	.922	.000	1.36	-0.015	2.84E-04
	200	.987	.000	1.05	-0.010	1.40E-04	.985	.000	1.17	-0.012	2.08E-04

Figure A3: CV (%) of the mean of random intercepts: average over Models 1 and 2 and both covariance cases (graphical representation of Table A4)

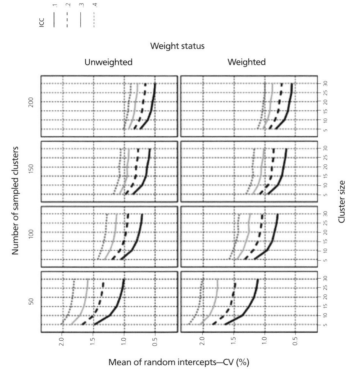

Table A5: Results of curve estimation for the CV (%) of the mean of random intercepts: quadratic equations (model summary and parameter estimates; average over Models 1 and 2 and both covariance cases; the independent variable is number of sampled clusters)

ICC	Cluster size	Weight status									
		Unweighted					Weighted				
		Model summary		Parameter estimates			Model summary		Parameter estimates		
		R square	Sig.	Constant	b1	b2	R square	Sig.	Constant	b1	b2
.1	5	.996	.000	2.04	-0.013	3.12E-05	.997	.000	2.26	-0.014	3.50E-05
	10	.997	.000	1.70	-0.011	2.62E-05	.996	.000	1.87	-0.012	2.87E-05
	15	.997	.000	1.55	-0.010	2.42E-05	.995	.000	1.72	-0.011	2.73E-05
	20	.993	.000	1.46	-0.009	2.23E-05	.996	.000	1.59	-0.010	2.32E-05
	25	.994	.000	1.41	-0.009	2.15E-05	.994	.000	1.54	-0.009	2.22E-05
	30	.994	.000	1.38	-0.009	2.09E-05	.996	.000	1.52	-0.009	2.32E-05
.2	5	.995	.000	2.31	-0.014	3.57E-05	.996	.000	2.50	-0.015	3.65E-05
	10	.997	.000	2.05	-0.013	3.13E-05	.999	.000	2.28	-0.014	3.56E-05
	15	.997	.000	1.95	-0.012	3.08E-05	.997	.000	2.15	-0.014	3.37E-05
	20	.993	.000	1.88	-0.012	2.87E-05	.994	.000	2.10	-0.013	3.30E-05
	25	.994	.000	1.84	-0.011	2.77E-05	.995	.000	2.04	-0.013	3.12E-05
	30	.994	.000	1.82	-0.011	2.75E-05	.994	.000	2.00	-0.012	2.97E-05
.3	5	.995	.000	2.56	-0.016	3.98E-05	.995	.000	2.80	-0.017	4.31E-05
	10	.997	.000	2.35	-0.014	3.56E-05	.996	.000	2.59	-0.016	3.93E-05
	15	.997	.000	2.29	-0.014	3.61E-05	.996	.000	2.50	-0.016	3.83E-05
	20	.993	.000	2.22	-0.014	3.41E-05	.990	.000	2.45	-0.015	3.89E-05
	25	.994	.000	2.19	-0.014	3.28E-05	.996	.000	2.41	-0.015	3.56E-05
	30	.994	.000	2.18	-0.013	3.29E-05	.994	.000	2.45	-0.016	3.96E-05
.4	5	.995	.000	2.79	-0.018	4.35E-05	.994	.000	3.05	-0.019	4.65E-05
	10	.996	.000	2.62	-0.016	3.94E-05	.997	.000	2.89	-0.018	4.31E-05
	15	.997	.000	2.58	-0.016	4.08E-05	.997	.000	2.84	-0.018	4.49E-05
	20	.993	.000	2.52	-0.016	3.86E-05	.991	.000	2.79	-0.017	4.32E-05
	25	.994	.000	2.49	-0.015	3.73E-05	.994	.000	2.78	-0.017	4.14E-05
	30	.993	.000	2.48	-0.015	3.75E-05	.994	.000	2.75	-0.017	4.23E-05

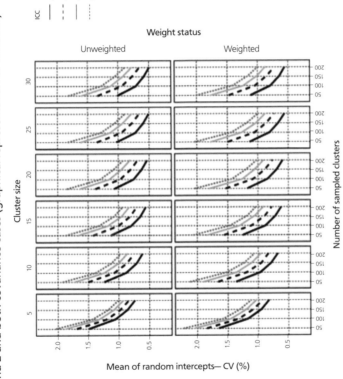

Figure A4: CV (%) of the mean of random intercepts: average over Models 1 and 2 and both covariance cases (graphical representation of Table A5)

Table A6: Results of curve estimation for the CV (%) of the mean of random intercepts: quadratic equations (model summary and parameter estimates, average over Models 3 and 4; the independent variable is cluster size)

Case	ICC	Number of sampled clusters	Unweighted					Weighted				
			Model summary		Parameter estimates			Model summary		Parameter estimates		
			R square	Sig.	Constant	b1	b2	R square	Sig.	Constant	b1	b2
Covariance Case 1 (20 at within and 10 at between level)	.1	50	.984	.000	1.67	-0.062	1.19E-03	0.985	.000	1.84	-0.068	1.32E-03
		100	.979	.000	1.15	-0.040	7.60E-04	0.977	.000	1.26	-0.044	8.34E-04
		150	.972	.000	0.93	-0.033	6.34E-04	0.972	.000	1.02	-0.035	6.49E-04
		200	.983	.000	0.80	-0.027	5.12E-04	0.981	.000	0.89	-0.032	6.12E-04
	.2	50	.982	.000	1.83	-0.046	8.85E-04	0.888	.000	1.98	-0.050	9.97E-04
		100	.980	.000	1.25	-0.029	5.47E-04	0.978	.000	1.39	-0.033	6.17E-04
		150	.965	.000	1.02	-0.024	4.73E-04	0.959	.000	1.15	-0.029	5.95E-04
		200	.982	.000	0.88	-0.019	3.50E-04	0.988	.000	0.96	-0.021	3.81E-04
	.3	50	.981	.000	1.98	-0.036	6.88E-04	0.980	.000	2.19	-0.040	7.93E-04
		100	.982	.000	1.36	-0.021	3.96E-04	0.975	.000	1.48	-0.022	3.98E-04
		150	.957	.000	1.11	-0.019	3.63E-04	0.966	.000	1.21	-0.018	3.25E-04
		200	.979	.000	0.95	-0.014	2.41E-04	0.968	.000	1.05	-0.017	3.11E-04
Covariance Case 2 (10 at within and 20 at between level)	.2	50	.987	.000	1.78	-0.068	1.30E-03	0.984	.000	1.95	-0.074	1.40E-03
		100	.982	.000	1.22	-0.044	8.20E-04	0.979	.000	1.35	-0.049	9.14E-04
		150	.975	.000	0.99	-0.036	6.83E-04	0.973	.000	1.11	-0.043	8.45E-04
		200	.988	.000	0.85	-0.030	5.57E-04	0.987	.000	0.93	-0.033	6.12E-04
	.3	50	.987	.000	1.93	-0.053	1.02E-03	0.983	.000	2.13	-0.059	1.14E-03
		100	.980	.000	1.32	-0.033	6.19E-04	0.981	.000	1.43	-0.033	6.15E-04
		150	.973	.000	1.07	-0.027	5.24E-04	0.971	.000	1.18	-0.029	5.37E-04
		200	.984	.000	0.92	-0.022	4.01E-04	0.979	.000	1.02	-0.025	4.79E-04
	.4	50	.985	.000	2.08	-0.042	8.18E-04	0.974	.000	2.31	-0.048	9.43E-04
		100	.979	.000	1.42	-0.025	4.75E-04	0.977	.000	1.56	-0.028	5.06E-04
		150	.966	.000	1.16	-0.022	4.20E-04	0.953	.000	1.28	-0.023	4.37E-04
		200	.979	.000	0.99	-0.017	2.96E-04	0.987	.000	1.10	-0.020	3.64E-04

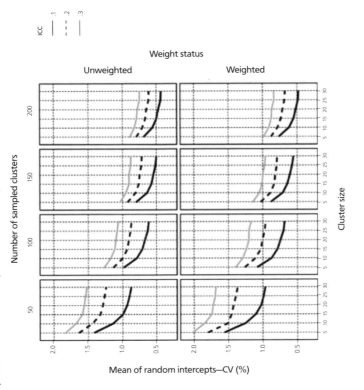

Figure A5: CV (%) of the mean of random intercepts: average over Models 3 and 4, Covariance Case 1 (20 at within and 10 at between level; graphical representation of first part of Table A6)

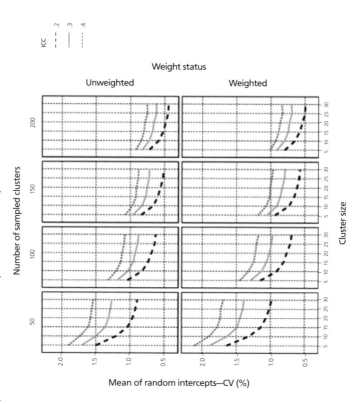

Figure A6: CV (%) of the mean of random intercepts: average over Models 3 and 4, Covariance Case 2 (10 at within and 20 at between level; graphical representation of second part of Table A6)

Table A7: Results of curve estimation for the CV (%) of the mean of random intercepts: quadratic equations (model summary and parameter estimates, average over Models 3 and 4; the independent variable is number of sampled clusters)

Covariance structure	ICC	Cluster size	Unweighted					Weighted				
			Model summary		Parameter estimates			Model summary		Parameter estimates		
			R square	Sig.	Constant	b1	b2	R square	Sig.	Constant	b1	b2
Covariance Case 1 (20 at within and 10 at between level)	.1	5	.995	.000	1.96	-0.013	3.15E-05	.995	.000	2.17	-0.014	3.57E-05
		10	.996	.000	1.60	-0.011	2.72E-05	.996	.000	1.75	-0.011	2.91E-05
		15	.997	.000	1.37	-0.009	2.15E-05	.995	.000	1.51	-0.009	2.29E-05
		20	.997	.000	1.28	-0.008	1.95E-05	.997	.000	1.39	-0.008	1.99E-05
		25	.994	.000	1.24	-0.008	1.97E-05	.994	.000	1.35	-0.008	2.06E-05
		30	.995	.000	1.20	-0.008	1.92E-05	.997	.000	1.33	-0.008	2.11E-05
	.2	5	.994	.000	2.27	-0.015	3.70E-05	.994	.000	2.47	-0.016	3.85E-05
		10	.996	.000	2.01	-0.013	3.35E-05	.984	.000	2.05	-0.012	2.99E-05
		15	.996	.000	1.83	-0.012	2.95E-05	.997	.000	2.01	-0.013	3.26E-05
		20	.995	.000	1.76	-0.011	2.76E-05	.996	.000	1.97	-0.013	3.12E-05
		25	.994	.000	1.74	-0.011	2.70E-05	.995	.000	1.91	-0.012	3.01E-05
		30	.994	.000	1.70	-0.011	2.67E-05	.994	.000	1.87	-0.012	2.92E-05
	3	5	.994	.000	2.54	-0.017	4.18E-05	.993	.000	2.81	-0.018	4.71E-05
		10	.995	.000	2.33	-0.015	3.81E-05	.995	.000	2.56	-0.017	4.18E-05
		15	.997	.000	2.20	-0.014	3.57E-05	.996	.000	2.39	-0.015	3.66E-05
		20	.994	.000	2.14	-0.013	3.36E-05	.992	.000	2.38	-0.015	3.89E-05
		25	.994	.000	2.12	-0.013	3.26E-05	.997	.000	2.32	-0.014	3.51E-05
		30	.993	.000	2.09	-0.013	3.25E-05	.994	.000	2.35	-0.015	3.93E-05

Weight status

Table A7: Results of curve estimation for the CV (%) of the mean of random intercepts: quadratic equations (model summary and parameter estimates, average over Models 3 and 4; the independent variable is number of sampled clusters) (contd.)

Covariance structure	ICC	Cluster size	Weight status										
			Unweighted					Weighted					
			Model summary		Parameter estimates			Model summary		Parameter estimates			
			R square	Sig.	Constant	b1	b2	R square	Sig.	Constant	b1	b2	
Covariance Case 2 (10 at within and 20 at between level)	.2	5	.994	.000	2.07	-0.013	3.36E-05	.994	.000	2.26	-0.014	3.48E-05	
		10	.997	.000	1.69	-0.011	2.95E-05	.997	.000	1.85	-0.012	3.15E-05	
		15	.997	.000	1.42	-0.009	2.19E-05	.997	.000	1.58	-0.010	2.55E-05	
		20	.997	.000	1.32	-0.008	2.03E-05	.998	.000	1.47	-0.009	2.31E-05	
		25	.994	.000	1.28	-0.008	2.06E-05	.994	.000	1.41	-0.009	2.28E-05	
		30	.996	.000	1.24	-0.008	2.00E-05	.994	.000	1.36	-0.009	2.21E-05	
	.3	5	.994	.000	2.38	-0.016	3.90E-05	.993	.000	2.64	-0.017	4.46E-05	
		10	.996	.000	2.10	-0.014	3.60E-05	.996	.000	2.29	-0.015	3.88E-05	
		15	.997	.000	1.87	-0.012	3.01E-05	.997	.000	2.03	-0.013	3.09E-05	
		20	.996	.000	1.79	-0.011	2.79E-05	.996	.000	1.99	-0.013	3.18E-05	
		25	.994	.000	1.77	-0.011	2.81E-05	.997	.000	1.94	-0.012	3.04E-05	
		30	.995	.000	1.73	-0.011	2.79E-05	.996	.000	1.93	-0.013	3.25E-05	
	.4	5	.994	.000	2.64	-0.017	4.36E-05	.993	.000	2.94	-0.019	4.89E-05	
		10	.996	.000	2.43	-0.016	4.13E-05	.996	.000	2.63	-0.017	4.31E-05	
		15	.996	.000	2.23	-0.014	3.64E-05	.996	.000	2.47	-0.016	4.03E-05	
		20	.996	.000	2.16	-0.014	3.39E-05	.993	.000	2.37	-0.015	3.63E-05	
		25	.995	.000	2.15	-0.014	3.38E-05	.994	.000	2.38	-0.015	3.64E-05	
		30	.994	.000	2.12	-0.013	3.37E-05	.994	.000	2.34	-0.015	3.84E-05	

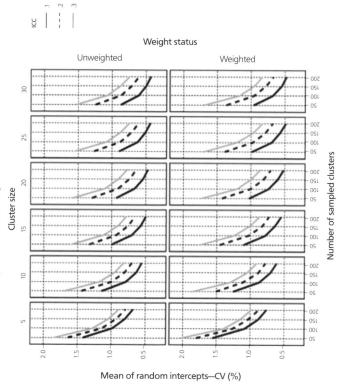

Figure A7: CV (%) of the mean of random intercepts: average over Models 3 and 4, Covariance Case 1 (20 at within and 10 at between level; graphical representation of first part of Table A7)

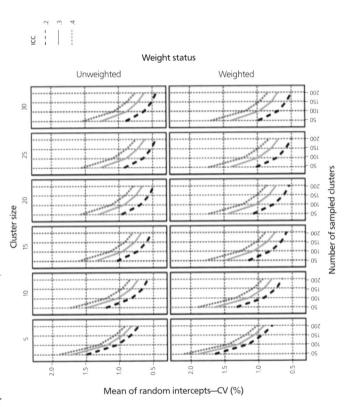

Figure A8: CV (%) of the mean of random intercepts: average over Models 3 and 4, Covariance Case 1 (20 at within and 10 at between level; graphical representation of second part of Table A7)

Table A8: Results of curve estimation for the CV (%) of the variance of random intercepts: quadratic equations (model summary and parameter estimates, Model 1; the independent variable is cluster size)

ICC	Number of sampled clusters	Weight status										
		Unweighted					Weighted					
		Model summary		Parameter estimates			Model summary		Parameter estimates			
		R square	Sig.	Constant	b1	b2	R square	Sig.	Constant	b1	b2	
.1	50	.958	.009	71.3	-3.73	0.076	.965	.006	79.9	-4.09	0.081	
	100	.942	.014	51.1	-2.75	0.056	.953	.010	59.2	-3.20	0.065	
	150	.939	.015	40.8	-2.18	0.045	.953	.010	47.4	-2.54	0.052	
	200	.945	.013	34.3	-1.77	0.036	.956	.009	41.1	-2.20	0.045	
.2	50	.954	.000	44.1	-1.72	0.035	.931	.000	48.8	-1.99	0.042	
	100	.951	.000	30.2	-1.12	0.022	.934	.000	33.4	-1.27	0.026	
	150	.952	.000	24.6	-0.93	0.019	.937	.000	27.2	-1.05	0.022	
	200	.959	.000	21.5	-0.81	0.016	.962	.000	24.2	-0.97	0.020	
.3	50	.955	.000	34.3	-1.00	0.020	.916	.000	36.6	-1.11	0.025	
	100	.937	.000	23.5	-0.65	0.013	.843	.000	27.1	-1.07	0.030	
	150	.943	.000	19.1	-0.53	0.011	.961	.000	22.0	-0.93	0.029	
	200	.956	.000	16.8	-0.47	0.009	.990	.000	19.4	-0.86	0.029	
.4	50	.953	.010	29.1	-0.62	0.012	.670	.190	29.9	-0.45	0.007	
	100	.917	.024	20.1	-0.40	0.008	.854	.056	21.6	-0.47	0.010	
	150	.932	.018	16.3	-0.33	0.006	.912	.026	17.5	-0.37	0.008	
	200	.954	.010	14.4	-0.29	0.005	.613	.241	14.7	-0.24	0.006	

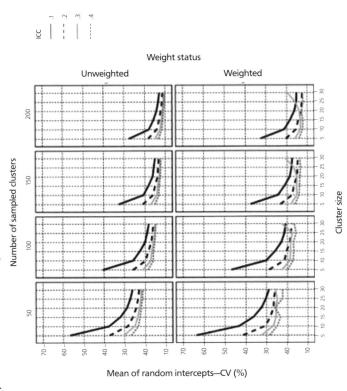

Figure A9: CV (%) of the variance of random intercepts: Model 1 (graphical representation of Table A8)

Table A9: Results of curve estimation for the CV (%) of the variance of random intercepts: quadratic equations (model summary and parameter estimates, Model 1; the independent variable is number of sampled clusters)

ICC	Cluster size	Weight status										
		Unweighted					Weighted					
		Model summary		Parameter estimates			Model summary		Parameter estimates			
		R square	Sig.	Constant	b1	b2	R square	Sig.	Constant	b1	b2	
.1	5	.998	.047	77.2	-0.469	1.11E-03	.999	.029	85.8	-0.504	1.19E-03	
	10	.996	.062	53.1	-0.357	9.16E-04	.996	.062	60.3	-0.396	1.01E-03	
	15	.997	.058	43.9	-0.275	6.79E-04	.997	.058	49.4	-0.304	7.51E-04	
	20	.996	.062	40.2	-0.264	6.75E-04	.996	.061	45.0	-0.290	7.36E-04	
	25	.994	.076	37.2	-0.234	5.78E-04	.993	.081	41.5	-0.260	6.51E-04	
	30	.993	.085	35.9	-0.227	5.66E-04	.995	.074	38.8	-0.232	5.74E-04	
.2	5	.995	.000	52.3	-0.346	8.89E-04	.996	.000	57.9	-0.384	9.86E-04	
	10	.996	.000	39.6	-0.260	6.69E-04	.997	.000	42.7	-0.282	7.29E-04	
	15	.997	.000	35.4	-0.217	5.27E-04	.997	.000	38.1	-0.228	5.51E-04	
	20	.996	.000	33.9	-0.222	5.68E-04	.996	.000	36.9	-0.236	5.81E-04	
	25	.994	.000	32.2	-0.202	4.98E-04	.994	.000	36.9	-0.242	6.07E-04	
	30	.993	.000	31.5	-0.199	4.94E-04	.991	.000	35.6	-0.231	5.84E-04	
.3	5	.996	.000	42.3	-0.278	7.11E-04	.997	.000	45.3	-0.300	7.70E-04	
	10	.995	.000	35.0	-0.233	6.01E-04	.996	.000	37.2	-0.242	6.14E-04	
	15	.997	.000	32.3	-0.198	4.81E-04	.994	.000	34.4	-0.206	5.07E-04	
	20	.996	.000	31.5	-0.205	5.24E-04	.998	.000	35.4	-0.226	5.96E-04	
	25	.994	.000	30.4	-0.191	4.71E-04	.962	.000	33.9	-0.220	6.57E-04	
	30	.993	.000	29.9	-0.190	4.71E-04	.997	.000	30.1	-0.096	2.22E-04	
.4	5	.996	.063	37.2	-0.243	6.21E-04	.996	.066	39.8	-0.260	6.59E-04	
	10	.994	.074	32.7	-0.218	5.65E-04	.994	.077	34.8	-0.230	5.90E-04	
	15	.996	.059	30.7	-0.189	4.58E-04	.996	.063	31.8	-0.195	4.85E-04	
	20	.996	.066	30.5	-0.199	5.08E-04	.995	.070	38.3	-0.290	8.17E-04	
	25	.994	.076	29.5	-0.186	4.58E-04	.992	.091	30.8	-0.200	5.34E-04	
	30	.994	.080	29.1	-0.184	4.57E-04	.998	.040	30.1	-0.179	4.52E-04	

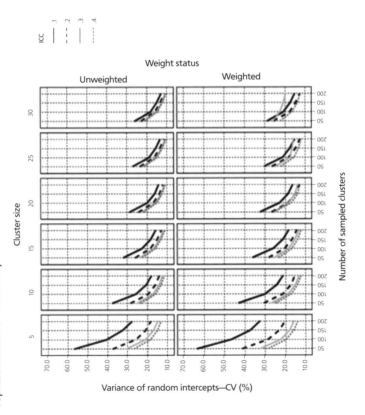

Figure A10: CV (%) of the variance of random intercepts: Model 1 (graphical representation of Table A9)

Table A10: Results of curve estimation for the CV (%) of the variance of random intercepts: quadratic equations (model summary and parameter estimates, Model 2; the independent variable is cluster size)

Covariance structure	ICC	Number of sampled clusters	Weight status										
			Unweighted					Weighted					
			Model summary		Parameter estimates			Model summary		Parameter estimates			
			R square	Sig.	Constant	b1	b2	R square	Sig.	Constant	b1	b2	
Covariance Case 1 (20 at within and 10 at between level)	.1	50	.954	.010	86.2	-4.977	0.102	.959	.008	92.8	-5.230	0.106	
		100	.935	.017	65.6	-4.014	0.084	.935	.016	72.2	-4.414	0.092	
		150	.927	.020	54.2	-3.384	0.071	.931	.018	59.1	-3.653	0.077	
		200	.930	.019	47.0	-2.914	0.061	.929	.019	52.1	-3.242	0.068	
	.2	50	.950	.011	47.9	-2.085	0.043	.937	.016	52.9	-2.289	0.047	
		100	.945	.013	32.6	-1.347	0.027	.939	.015	36.3	-1.500	0.030	
		150	.945	.013	26.6	-1.112	0.023	.938	.016	29.3	-1.224	0.025	
		200	.952	.010	23.1	-0.957	0.019	.952	.011	25.8	-1.102	0.022	
	.3	50	.959	.008	36.4	-1.336	0.032	.950	.011	39.6	-1.369	0.031	
		100	.865	.050	26.7	-1.194	0.033	.912	.026	29.2	-1.237	0.033	
		150	.922	.022	22.5	-1.150	0.034	.941	.014	24.2	-1.144	0.033	
		200	.937	.016	20.2	-1.099	0.033	.960	.008	21.6	-1.096	0.033	

Table A10: Results of curve estimation for the CV (%) of the variance of random intercepts: quadratic equations (model summary and parameter estimates, Model 2; the independent variable is cluster size) (contd.)

Covariance structure	ICC	Number of sampled clusters	Weight status										
			Unweighted					Weighted					
			Model summary		Parameter estimates			Model summary		Parameter estimates			
			R square	Sig.	Constant	b1	b2	R square	Sig.	Constant	b1	b2
Covariance Case 2 (10 at within and 20 at between level)	.2	50	.941	.014	52.4	-2.460	0.051	.929	.019	58.1	-2.733	0.057
		100	.939	.015	35.9	-1.626	0.033	.931	.018	40.0	-1.819	0.037
		150	.937	.016	29.2	-1.343	0.028	.930	.019	32.3	-1.481	0.031
		200	.945	.013	25.4	-1.155	0.023	.945	.013	28.4	-1.323	0.027
	.3	50	.951	.011	37.2	-1.279	0.027	.945	.013	40.9	-1.394	0.029
		100	.944	.013	26.1	-0.936	0.021	.961	.008	28.9	-1.041	0.023
		150	.950	.011	21.5	-0.828	0.020	.957	.009	23.4	-0.864	0.020
		200	.964	.007	18.9	-0.735	0.017	.956	.009	20.6	-0.787	0.018
	.4	50	.546	.306	28.3	-0.370	0.005	.668	.192	32.1	-0.563	0.010
		100	.827	.072	21.0	-0.486	0.011	.853	.056	23.1	-0.520	0.011
		150	.869	.047	16.9	-0.371	0.008	.907	.029	18.8	-0.425	0.009
		200	.763	.115	14.7	-0.305	0.007	.782	.102	16.2	-0.339	0.007

Figure A11: CV (%) of the variance of random intercepts: Model 2, Covariance Case 1 (20 at within and 10 at between level; graphical representation of first part of Table A10)

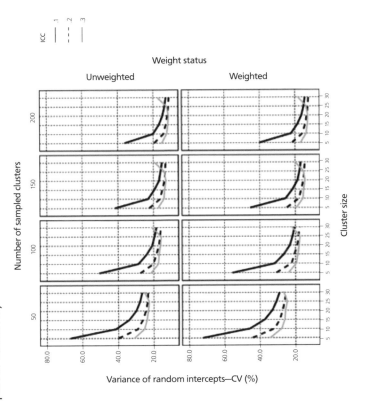

Figure A12: CV (%) of the variance of random intercepts: Model 2, Covariance Case 2 (10 at within and 20 at between level; graphical representation of second part of Table A10)

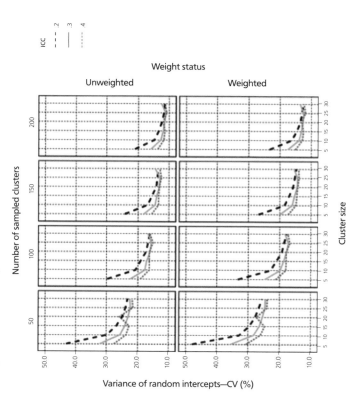

Table A11: Results of curve estimation for the CV (%) of the variance of random intercepts: quadratic equations (model summary and parameter estimates, Model 2; the independent variable is number of sampled clusters)

Covariance structure	ICC	Cluster size	Weight status									
			Unweighted					Weighted				
			Model summary		Parameter estimates			Model summary		Parameter estimates		
			R square	Sig.	Constant	b1	b2	R square	Sig.	Constant	b1	b2
Covariance Case 1 (20 at within and 10 at between level)	.1	5	.998	.040	87.7	-0.475	1.09E-03	1.000	.015	94.4	-0.499	1.14E-03
		10	.996	.059	57.9	-0.385	9.84E-04	.996	.062	64.4	-0.430	1.10E-03
		15	.997	.058	46.5	-0.291	7.16E-04	.997	.058	51.3	-0.322	7.97E-04
		20	.996	.061	41.7	-0.273	6.98E-04	.996	.063	46.0	-0.300	7.63E-04
		25	.994	.077	38.1	-0.239	5.91E-04	.996	.067	42.2	-0.266	6.60E-04
		30	.993	.085	36.5	-0.232	5.78E-04	.994	.078	39.4	-0.244	6.00E-04
	.2	5	.995	.071	55.8	-0.370	9.48E-04	.996	.062	61.9	-0.411	1.05E-03
		10	.996	.066	40.4	-0.267	6.86E-04	.997	.056	44.2	-0.290	7.41E-04
		15	.997	.058	35.8	-0.221	5.38E-04	.997	.053	39.4	-0.242	5.87E-04
		20	.996	.062	33.9	-0.222	5.67E-04	.994	.074	37.9	-0.246	6.22E-04
		25	.994	.076	32.2	-0.202	4.95E-04	.995	.071	35.8	-0.226	5.56E-04
		30	.992	.087	31.9	-0.205	5.14E-04	.991	.096	35.1	-0.227	5.75E-04
	.3	5	.996	.066	43.2	-0.283	7.24E-04	.997	.057	47.5	-0.310	7.90E-04
		10	.995	.072	35.3	-0.235	6.08E-04	.997	.056	38.5	-0.248	6.24E-04
		15	.997	.057	32.5	-0.199	4.82E-04	.996	.063	35.5	-0.216	5.23E-04
		20	.997	.051	31.9	-0.205	5.13E-04	.997	.055	35.7	-0.234	5.98E-04
		25	.982	.135	30.7	-0.194	5.20E-04	.984	.128	33.6	-0.211	5.65E-045
		30	.992	.090	29.9	-0.111	2.51E-04	.993	.084	32.0	-0.126	2.95E-04

Table A11: Results of curve estimation for the CV (%) of the variance of random intercepts: quadratic equations (model summary and parameter estimates, Model 2; the independent variable is number of sampled clusters) (contd.)

Covariance structure	ICC	Cluster size	Weight status										
			Unweighted					Weighted					
			Model summary		Parameter estimates			Model summary		Parameter estimates			
			R square	Sig.	Constant	b1	b2	R square	Sig.	Constant	b1	b2
Covariance Case 2 (10 at within and 20 at between level)	.2	5	.995	.070	60.2	-0.398	1.02E-03	.996	.061	67.0	-0.443	1.13E-03
		10	.996	.064	41.7	-0.275	7.07E-04	.997	.056	45.7	-0.301	7.72E-04
		15	.997	.057	36.6	-0.226	5.50E-04	.997	.051	40.3	-0.247	5.98E-04
		20	.996	.061	34.6	-0.226	5.78E-04	.995	.073	38.4	-0.249	6.27E-04
		25	.994	.078	32.7	-0.206	5.08E-04	.995	.073	36.5	-0.232	5.76E-04
		30	.993	.084	31.9	-0.202	5.03E-04	.991	.095	35.2	-0.226	5.71E-04
	.3	5	.996	.067	44.9	-0.295	7.55E-04	.997	.059	49.6	-0.325	8.29E-04
		10	.995	.070	35.8	-0.237	6.14E-04	.997	.055	39.0	-0.250	6.28E-04
		15	.997	.059	32.8	-0.202	4.90E-04	.995	.068	36.0	-0.224	5.52E-04
		20	.996	.067	32.0	-0.208	5.31E-04	.997	.054	35.3	-0.230	5.88E-04
		25	.994	.075	30.7	-0.195	4.92E-04	.992	.089	33.9	-0.217	5.54E-04
		30	.991	.093	29.4	-0.161	3.83E-04	.996	.064	32.4	-0.183	4.45E-04
	.4	5	.996	.064	38.4	-0.251	6.41E-04	.995	.068	42.5	-0.277	7.03E-04
		10	.995	.073	33.1	-0.220	5.72E-04	.994	.078	36.3	-0.239	6.13E-04
		15	.996	.063	30.8	-0.186	4.48E-04	.997	.052	33.4	-0.200	4.81E-04
		20	.992	.090	38.4	-0.298	8.35E-04	.995	.069	40.1	-0.300	8.29E-04
		25	.995	.073	29.6	-0.189	4.78E-04	.993	.085	33.1	-0.212	5.36E-04
		30	.999	.024	29.2	-0.169	4.00E-04	.999	.034	32.6	-0.201	4.99E-04

Figure A13: CV (%) of the variance of random intercepts: Model 2, Covariance Case 1 (20 at within and 10 at between level; graphical representation of first part of Table A11)

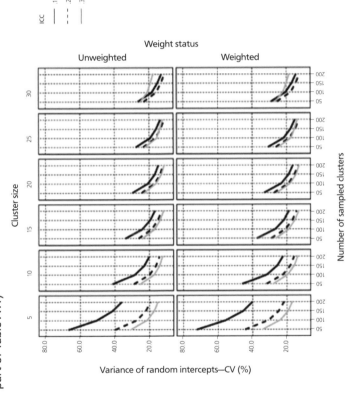

Figure A14: CV (%) of the variance of random intercepts: Model 2, Covariance Case 2 (10 at within and 20 at between level; graphical representation of second part of Table A11)

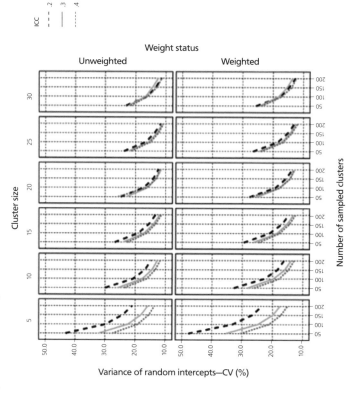

Table A12: Results of curve estimation for the CV (%) of the variance of random intercepts: quadratic equations (model summary and parameter estimates, Model 3; the independent variable is cluster size)

Covariance structure	ICC	Number of sampled clusters	Weight status									
			Unweighted					Weighted				
			Model summary		Parameter estimates			Model summary		Parameter estimates		
			R square	Sig.	Constant	b1	b2	R square	Sig.	Constant	b1	b2
Covariance Case 1 (20 at within and 10 at between level)	.1	50	.954	.010	86.2	-4.977	0.102	.959	.008	92.8	-5.230	0.106
		100	.935	.017	65.6	-4.014	0.084	.935	.016	72.2	-4.414	0.092
		150	.927	.020	54.2	-3.384	0.071	.931	.018	59.1	-3.653	0.077
		200	.930	.019	47.0	-2.914	0.061	.929	.019	52.1	-3.242	0.068
	.2	50	.950	.011	47.9	-2.085	0.043	.937	.016	52.9	-2.289	0.047
		100	.945	.013	32.6	-1.347	0.027	.939	.015	36.3	-1.500	0.030
		150	.945	.013	26.6	-1.112	0.023	.938	.016	29.3	-1.224	0.025
		200	.952	.010	23.1	-0.957	0.019	.952	.011	25.8	-1.102	0.022
	.3	50	.959	.008	36.4	-1.336	0.032	.950	.011	39.6	-1.369	0.031
		100	.865	.050	26.7	-1.194	0.033	.912	.026	29.2	-1.237	0.033
		150	.922	.022	22.5	-1.150	0.034	.941	.014	24.2	-1.144	0.033
		200	.937	.016	20.2	-1.099	0.033	.960	.008	21.6	-1.096	0.033

Table A12: Results of curve estimation for the CV (%) of the variance of random intercepts: quadratic equations (model summary and parameter estimates, Model 3; the independent variable is cluster size) (contd.)

Covariance structure	ICC	Number of sampled clusters	Weight status									
			Unweighted					Weighted				
			Model summary		Parameter estimates			Model summary		Parameter estimates		
			R square	Sig.	Constant	b1	b2	R square	Sig.	Constant	b1	b2
Covariance Case 2 (10 at within and 20 at between level)	.2	50	.941	.014	52.4	-2.460	0.051	.929	.019	58.1	-2.733	0.057
		100	.939	.015	35.9	-1.626	0.033	.931	.018	40.0	-1.819	0.037
		150	.937	.016	29.2	-1.343	0.028	.930	.019	32.3	-1.481	0.031
		200	.945	.013	25.4	-1.155	0.023	.945	.013	28.4	-1.323	0.027
	.3	50	.951	.011	37.2	-1.279	0.027	.945	.013	40.9	-1.394	0.029
		100	.944	.013	26.1	-0.936	0.021	.961	.008	28.9	-1.041	0.023
		150	.950	.011	21.5	-0.828	0.020	.957	.009	23.4	-.0864	0.020
		200	.964	.007	18.9	-0.735	0.017	.956	.009	20.6	-0.787	0.018
	.4	50	.546	.306	28.3	-0.370	0.005	.668	.192	32.1	-0.563	0.010
		100	.827	.072	21.0	-0.486	0.011	.853	.056	23.1	-0.520	0.011
		150	.869	.047	16.9	-0.371	0.008	.907	.029	18.8	-0.425	0.009
		200	.763	.115	14.7	-0.305	0.007	.782	.102	16.2	-0.339	0.007

Figure A15: CV (%) of the variance of random intercepts: Model 3, Covariance Case 1 (20 at within and 10 at between level; graphical representation of first part of Table A12)

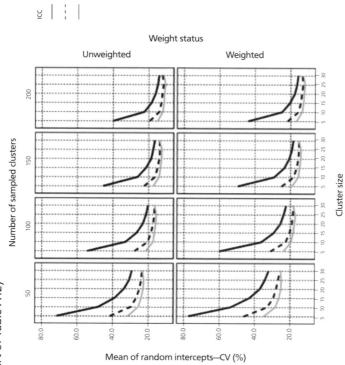

Figure A16: CV (%) of the variance of random intercepts: Model 3, Covariance Case 2 (10 at within and 20 at between level; graphical representation of second part of Table A12)

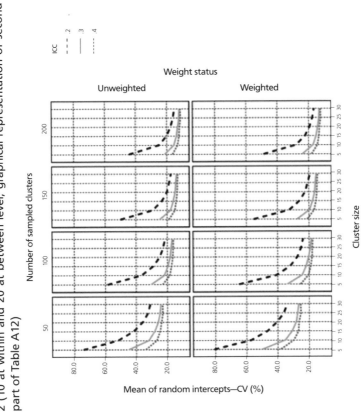

Table A13: Results of curve estimation for the CV (%) of the variance of random intercepts: quadratic equations (model summary and parameter estimates, Model 3; the independent variable is number of sampled clusters)

Covariance structure	ICC	Cluster size	Weight status									
			Unweighted					Weighted				
			Model summary		Parameter estimates			Model summary		Parameter estimates		
			R square	Sig.	Constant	b1	b2	R square	Sig.	Constant	b1	b2
Covariance Case 1 (20 at within and 10 at between level)	.1	5	.998	.040	87.7	-0.475	1.09E-03	1.000	.015	94.4	-0.499	1.14E-03
		10	.996	.059	57.9	-0.385	9.84E-04	.996	.062	64.4	-0.430	1.10E-03
		15	.997	.058	46.5	-0.291	7.16E-04	.997	.058	51.3	-0.322	7.97E-04
		20	.996	.061	41.7	-0.273	6.98E-04	.996	.063	46.0	-0.300	7.63E-04
		25	.994	.077	38.1	-0.239	5.91E-04	.996	.067	42.2	-0.266	6.60E-04
		30	.993	.085	36.5	-0.232	5.78E-04	.994	.078	39.4	-0.244	6.00E-04
	.2	5	.995	.071	55.8	-0.370	9.48E-04	.996	.062	61.9	-0.411	1.05E-03
		10	.996	.066	40.4	-0.267	6.86E-04	.997	.056	44.2	-0.290	7.41E-04
		15	.997	.058	35.8	-0.221	5.38E-04	.997	.053	39.4	-0.242	5.87E-04
		20	.996	.062	33.9	-0.222	5.67E-04	.994	.074	37.9	-0.246	6.22E-04
		25	.994	.076	32.2	-0.202	4.95E-04	.995	.071	35.8	-0.226	5.56E-04
		30	.992	.087	31.9	-0.205	5.14E-04	.991	.096	35.1	-0.227	5.75E-04
	.3	5	.996	.066	43.2	-0.283	7.24E-04	.997	.057	47.5	-0.310	7.90E-04
		10	.995	.072	35.3	-0.235	6.08E-04	.997	.056	38.5	-0.248	6.24E-04
		15	.997	.057	32.5	-0.199	4.82E-04	.996	.063	35.5	-0.216	5.23E-04
		20	.997	.051	31.9	-0.205	5.13E-04	.997	.055	35.7	-0.234	5.98E-04
		25	.982	.135	30.7	-0.194	5.20E-04	.984	.128	33.6	-0.211	5.65E-045
		30	.992	.090	29.9	-0.111	2.51E-04	.993	.084	32.0	-0.126	2.95E-04

Table A13: Results of curve estimation for the CV (%) of the variance of random intercepts: quadratic equations (model summary and parameter estimates, Model 3; the independent variable is number of sampled clusters) (contd.)

Covariance structure	ICC	Cluster size	Unweighted					Weighted				
			Model summary		Parameter estimates			Model summary		Parameter estimates		
			R square	Sig.	Constant	b1	b2	R square	Sig.	Constant	b1	b2
Covariance Case 2 (10 at within and 20 at between level)	.2	5	.995	.070	60.2	-0.398	1.02E-03	.996	.061	67.0	-0.443	1.13E-03
		10	.996	.064	41.7	-0.275	7.07E-04	.997	.056	45.7	-0.301	7.72E-04
		15	.997	.057	36.6	-0.226	5.50E-04	.997	.051	40.3	-0.247	5.98E-04
		20	.996	.061	34.6	-0.226	5.78E-04	.995	.073	38.4	-0.249	6.27E-04
		25	.994	.078	32.7	-0.206	5.08E-04	.995	.073	36.5	-0.232	5.76E-04
		30	.993	.084	31.9	-0.202	5.03E-04	.991	.095	35.2	-0.226	5.71E-04
	.3	5	.996	.067	44.9	-0.295	7.55E-04	.997	.059	49.6	-0.325	8.29E-04
		10	.995	.070	35.8	-0.237	6.14E-04	.997	.055	39.0	-0.250	6.28E-04
		15	.997	.059	32.8	-0.202	4.90E-04	.995	.068	36.0	-0.224	5.52E-04
		20	.996	.067	32.0	-0.208	5.31E-04	.997	.054	35.3	-0.230	5.88E-04
		25	.994	.075	30.7	-0.195	4.92E-04	.992	.089	33.9	-0.217	5.54E-04
		30	.991	.093	29.4	-0.161	3.83E-04	.996	.064	32.4	-0.183	4.45E-04
	.4	5	.996	.064	38.4	-0.251	6.41E-04	.995	.068	42.5	-0.277	7.03E-04
		10	.995	.073	33.1	-0.220	5.72E-04	.994	.078	36.3	-0.239	6.13E-04
		15	.996	.063	30.8	-0.186	4.48E-04	.997	.052	33.4	-0.200	4.81E-04
		20	.992	.090	38.4	-0.298	8.35E-04	.995	.069	40.1	-0.300	8.29E-04
		25	.995	.073	29.6	-0.189	4.78E-04	.993	.085	33.1	-0.212	5.36E-04
		30	.999	.024	29.2	-0.169	4.00E-04	.999	.034	32.6	-0.201	4.99E-04

Figure A17: CV (%) of the variance of random intercepts: Model 3, Covariance Case 1 (20 at within and 10 at between level; graphical representation of first part of Table A13)

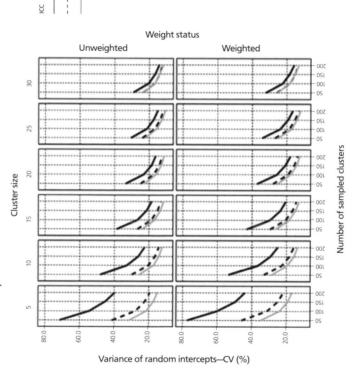

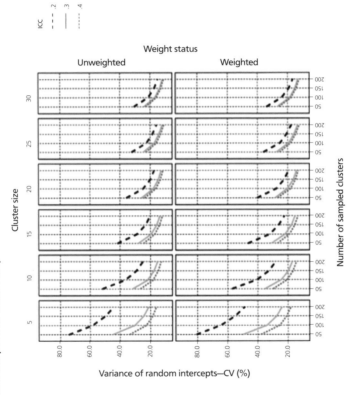

Figure A18: CV (%) of the variance of random intercepts: Model 3, Covariance Case 2 (10 at within and 20 at between level; graphical representation of second part of Table A13)

Table A14: Results of curve estimation for the CV (%) of the variance of random intercepts: quadratic equations (model summary and parameter estimates, Model 4; the independent variable is cluster size)

Covariance structure	ICC	Number of sampled clusters	Weight status										
			Unweighted					Weighted					
			Model summary		Parameter estimates			Model summary		Parameter estimates			
			R square	Sig.	Constant	b1	b2	R square	Sig.	Constant	b1	b2	
Covariance Case 1 (20 at within and 10 at between level)	.1	50	.971	.005	107.1	-6.20	0.124	.974	.004	117.4	-6.71	0.133	
		100	.958	.009	76.6	-4.60	0.094	.957	.009	85.4	-5.15	0.105	
		150	.950	.011	62.1	-3.78	0.078	.955	.010	68.4	-4.16	0.086	
		200	.949	.012	53.9	-3.29	0.068	.951	.011	59.8	-3.68	0.076	
	.2	50	.947	.012	54.0	-2.53	0.052	.857	.054	59.4	-2.87	0.061	
		100	.944	.013	35.2	-1.53	0.031	.945	.013	39.6	-1.76	0.036	
		150	.943	.014	28.4	-1.24	0.026	.941	.014	31.4	-1.37	0.028	
		200	.947	.012	24.4	-1.05	0.021	.946	.012	27.3	-1.20	0.025	
	.3	50	.946	.013	37.9	-1.29	0.026	.949	.012	42.0	-1.46	0.030	
		100	.934	.017	25.1	-0.78	0.016	.945	.013	27.9	-0.86	0.017	
		150	.936	.016	20.3	-0.63	0.013	.931	.018	22.4	-0.69	0.014	
		200	.951	.011	17.6	-0.54	0.011	.942	.014	19.6	-0.62	0.013	

Table A14: Results of curve estimation for the CV (%) of the variance of random intercepts: quadratic equations (model summary and parameter estimates, Model 4; the independent variable is cluster size) (contd.)

Covariance structure	ICC	Number of sampled clusters	Weight status										
			Unweighted					Weighted					
			Model summary		Parameter estimates			Model summary		Parameter estimates			
			R square	Sig.	Constant	b1	b2	R square	Sig.	Constant	b1	b2	
Covariance Case 2 (10 at within and 20 at between level)	.2	50	.983	.002	110.3	-6.11	0.119	.984	.002	118.8	-6.37	0.121	
		100	.968	.006	83.4	-5.00	0.101	.970	.005	92.1	-5.51	0.111	
		150	.956	.009	69.9	-4.33	0.089	.955	.010	78.0	-4.84	0.099	
		200	.949	.011	61.0	-3.83	0.079	.952	.010	67.3	-4.21	0.086	
	.3	50	.953	.010	61.0	-3.09	0.064	.955	.009	67.5	-3.43	0.071	
		100	.948	.012	39.8	-1.90	0.039	.948	.012	44.4	-2.11	0.043	
		150	.943	.013	32.0	-1.52	0.032	.939	.015	35.6	-1.71	0.035	
		200	.946	.013	27.3	-1.29	0.026	.948	.012	30.7	-1.48	0.030	
	.4	50	.953	.010	42.5	-1.68	0.035	.956	.009	47.8	-1.96	0.041	
		100	.942	.014	27.6	-0.97	0.020	.943	.014	30.8	-1.11	0.023	
		150	.937	.016	22.2	-0.78	0.016	.937	.016	24.9	-0.90	0.018	
		200	.947	.012	19.1	-0.66	0.013	.942	.014	21.2	-0.74	0.015	

Figure A19: CV (%) of the variance of random intercepts: Model 4, Covariance Case 1 (20 at within and 10 at between level; graphical representation of first part of Table A14)

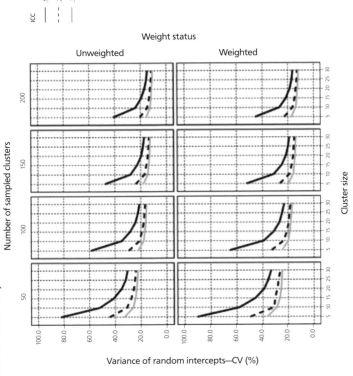

Figure A20: CV (%) ratio of the variance of random intercepts: Model 4, Covariance Case 2 (10 at within and 20 at between level; graphical representation of second part of Table A14)

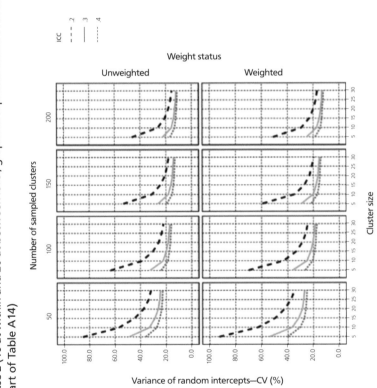

Table A15: Results of curve estimation for the CV (%) of the variance of random intercepts: quadratic equations (model summary and parameter estimates, Model 4; the independent variable is number of sampled clusters)

Covariance structure	ICC	Cluster size	Weight status										
			Unweighted					Weighted					
			Model summary		Parameter estimates			Model summary		Parameter estimates			
			R square	Sig.	Constant	b1	b2	R square	Sig.	Constant	b1	b2	
Covariance Case 1 (20 at within and 10 at between level)	.1	5	.997	.055	112.8	-0.702	1.73E-03	.999	.036	123.2	-0.752	1.83E-03	
		10	.996	.064	74.1	-0.510	1.31E-03	.995	.068	82.6	-0.568	1.45E-03	
		15	.995	.067	57.9	-0.386	9.74E-04	.996	.064	65.0	-0.443	1.13E-03	
		20	.996	.067	49.8	-0.336	8.64E-04	.995	.070	54.3	-0.358	9.03E-04	
		25	.994	.076	44.0	-0.281	6.95E-04	.996	.065	49.2	-0.316	7.78E-04	
		30	.994	.079	42.4	-0.279	7.08E-04	.993	.084	46.2	-0.301	7.60E-04	
	.2	5	.993	.084	63.5	-0.447	1.17E-03	.994	.078	71.3	-0.507	1.33E-03	
		10	.995	.072	43.8	-0.298	7.69E-04	1.000	.020	40.8	-0.221	4.94E-04	
		15	.995	.069	38.3	-0.247	6.17E-04	.995	.073	42.1	-0.273	6.84E-04	
		20	.996	.066	35.8	-0.238	6.13E-04	.994	.079	40.0	-0.268	6.89E-04	
		25	.994	.076	33.8	-0.215	5.26E-04	.993	.085	38.0	-0.244	6.00E-04	
		30	.993	.083	33.2	-0.216	5.47E-04	.993	.081	36.3	-0.234	5.91E-04	
	.3	5	.994	.078	46.7	-0.321	8.29E-04	.995	.070	51.5	-0.353	9.12E-04	
		10	.994	.074	36.8	-0.250	6.49E-04	.997	.057	40.5	-0.270	6.86E-04	
		15	.995	.067	33.6	-0.214	5.31E-04	.996	.066	36.5	-0.229	5.64E-04	
		20	.995	.069	32.5	-0.214	5.50E-04	.997	.056	35.4	-0.228	5.74E-04	
		25	.994	.076	31.3	-0.198	4.83E-04	.993	.082	34.7	-0.222	5.51E-04	
		30	.993	.083	30.8	-0.199	5.01E-04	.992	.089	34.2	-0.227	5.83E-04	

Table A15: Results of curve estimation for the CV (%) of the variance of random intercepts: quadratic equations (model summary and parameter estimates, Model 4; the independent variable is number of sampled clusters) (contd.)

Covariance structure	ICC	Cluster size	Unweighted					Weight status Weighted				
			Model summary		Parameter estimates			Model summary		Parameter estimates		
			R square	Sig.	Constant	b1	b2	R square	Sig.	Constant	b1	b2
Covariance Case 2 (10 at within and 20 at between level)	.2	5	.997	.056	112.4	-0.626	1.49E-03	.996	.062	120.1	-0.632	1.44E-03
		10	.996	.060	80.1	-0.535	1.34E-03	.996	.060	88.3	-0.585	1.46E-03
		15	.995	.068	62.6	-0.420	1.07E-03	.995	.073	70.2	-0.479	1.22E-03
		20	.996	.065	52.9	-0.357	9.18E-04	.995	.073	60.0	-0.412	1.06E-03
		25	.995	.070	46.6	-0.300	7.47E-04	.993	.083	52.0	-0.337	8.41E-04
		30	.996	.066	44.5	-0.293	7.40E-04	.997	.059	48.7	-0.315	7.86E-04
	.3	5	.993	.083	70.1	-0.492	1.28E-03	.994	.075	76.9	-0.532	1.37E-03
		10	.995	.071	46.9	-0.319	8.20E-04	.997	.058	51.9	-0.352	9.00E-04
		15	.995	.070	40.2	-0.264	6.66E-04	.997	.059	43.9	-0.283	7.05E-04
		20	.996	.060	36.5	-0.238	6.08E-04	.998	.045	39.6	-0.251	6.25E-04
		25	.995	.074	34.3	-0.215	5.26E-04	.994	.079	38.1	-0.240	5.86E-04
		30	.995	.074	34.1	-0.222	5.60E-04	.994	.078	37.8	-0.252	6.49E-04
	.4	5	.993	.083	51.4	-0.361	9.43E-04	.992	.090	57.3	-0.403	1.05E-03
		10	.995	.071	38.7	-0.263	6.81E-04	.994	.077	43.0	-0.292	7.51E-04
		15	.996	.067	34.8	-0.226	5.67E-04	.996	.064	37.6	-0.242	6.08E-04
		20	.996	.062	32.6	-0.211	5.38E-04	.995	.068	36.2	-0.238	6.12E-04
		25	.995	.074	31.6	-0.198	4.81E-04	.995	.074	34.6	-0.212	5.09E-04
		30	.994	.077	31.5	-0.205	5.18E-04	.994	.080	35.1	-0.233	6.00E-04

Figure A21: CV (%) of the variance of random intercepts: Model 4, Covariance Case 1 (20 at within and 10 at between level; graphical representation of first part of Table A15)

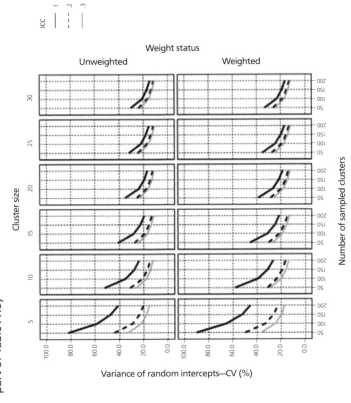

Figure A22: CV (%) of the variance of random intercepts: Model 4, Covariance Case 2 (10 at within and 20 at between level; graphical representation of second part of Table A15)

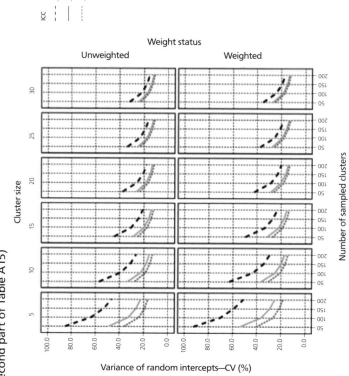

Table A16: Results of curve estimation for the CV (%) of the fixed slope: quadratic equations (model summary and parameter estimates, Model 2; the independent variable is cluster size)

Covariance structure	ICC	Number of sampled clusters	Weight status										
			Unweighted					Weighted					
			Model summary		Parameter estimates			Model summary		Parameter estimates			
			R square	Sig.	Constant	b1	b2	R square	Sig.	Constant	b1	b2	
Covariance Case 1 (20 at within and 10 at between level)	.1	50	.986	.002	30.3	-1.459	0.027	.986	.002	33.2	-1.586	0.029	
		100	.988	.001	21.3	-1.020	0.019	.988	.001	23.6	-1.133	0.021	
		150	.982	.003	17.6	-0.859	0.016	.984	.002	19.2	-0.921	0.017	
		200	.981	.003	14.9	-0.712	0.013	.983	.002	16.2	-0.756	0.014	
	.2	50	.984	.002	30.0	-1.507	0.028	.984	.002	32.6	-1.604	0.030	
		100	.985	.002	21.1	-1.049	0.019	.986	.002	23.2	-1.146	0.021	
		150	.979	.003	17.4	-0.879	0.016	.982	.002	19.1	-0.953	0.018	
		200	.979	.003	14.7	-0.730	0.014	.980	.003	16.1	-0.789	0.015	
	.3	50	.981	.003	28.9	-1.487	0.028	.979	.003	31.4	-1.591	0.030	
		100	.983	.002	20.3	-1.036	0.019	.980	.003	22.2	-1.126	0.021	
		150	.977	.003	16.7	-0.868	0.016	.980	.003	18.2	-0.930	0.017	
		200	.977	.004	14.2	-0.722	0.014	.978	.003	15.8	-0.804	0.015	
Covariance Case 2 (10 at within and 20 at between level)	.2	50	.997	.000	47.0	-1.774	0.029	.997	.000	50.9	-1.848	0.029	
		100	.998	.000	33.3	-1.260	0.020	.998	.000	36.6	-1.372	0.022	
		150	.995	.000	27.4	-1.052	0.017	.997	.000	30.0	-1.132	0.018	
		200	.994	.000	23.2	-0.867	0.014	.995	.000	25.5	-0.940	0.015	
	.3	50	.994	.000	48.5	-2.045	0.035	.992	.001	52.8	-2.184	0.037	
		100	.996	.000	34.4	-1.452	0.025	.994	.000	37.4	-1.559	0.027	
		150	.992	.001	28.2	-1.208	0.021	.994	.001	30.6	-1.275	0.022	
		200	.990	.001	24.0	-1.003	0.017	.991	.001	26.6	-1.113	0.019	
	.4	50	.991	.001	48.3	-2.193	0.039	.989	.001	53.4	-2.464	0.044	
		100	.993	.001	34.2	-1.553	0.028	.994	.000	37.0	-1.638	0.029	
		150	.988	.001	28.1	-1.291	0.023	.991	.001	30.4	-1.375	0.024	
		200	.987	.002	23.8	-1.076	0.019	.987	.001	26.5	-1.200	0.021	

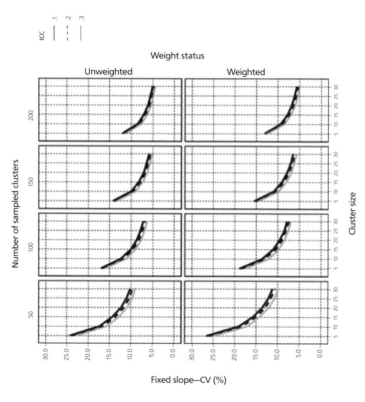

Figure A23: CV (%) of the fixed slope: Model 2, Covariance Case 1 (20 at within and 10 at between level; graphical representation of first part of Table A16)

Figure A24: CV (%) of the fixed slope: Model 2, Covariance Case 2 (10 at within and 20 at between level; graphical representation of second part of Table A16)

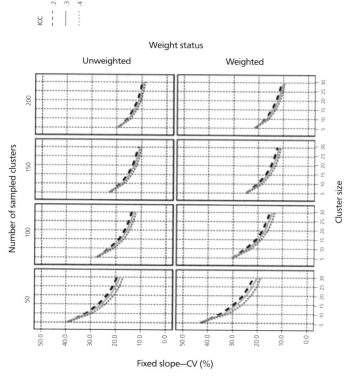

Table A17: Results of curve estimation for the CV (%) of the fixed slope: quadratic equations (model summary and parameter estimates, Model 2; the independent variable is number of sampled clusters)

Case	ICC	Cluster size	Weight status										
			Unweighted					Weighted					
			Model summary		Parameter estimates			Model summary		Parameter estimates			
			R square	Sig.	Constant	b1	b2	R square	Sig.	Constant	b1	b2	
Covariance Case 1 (20 at within and 10 at between level)	.1	5	.993	.084	33.1	-0.206	5.08E-04	.995	.068	36.2	-0.222	5.35E-04	
		10	.997	.055	23.7	-0.146	3.54E-04	.997	.056	26.1	-0.161	3.91E-04	
		15	.995	.073	19.8	-0.126	3.18E-04	.995	.067	21.6	-0.136	3.36E-04	
		20	.996	.067	16.8	-0.106	2.63E-04	.995	.069	18.5	-0.115	2.86E-04	
		25	.995	.069	14.9	-0.092	2.26E-04	.994	.076	16.7	-0.107	2.75E-04	
		30	.995	.068	14.0	-0.088	2.20E-04	.995	.072	15.3	-0.096	2.38E-04	
	.2	5	.993	.083	32.6	-0.204	5.03E-04	.994	.076	35.3	-0.216	5.25E-04	
		10	.997	.055	22.7	-0.140	3.39E-04	.997	.058	24.9	-0.151	3.61E-04	
		15	.995	.073	18.8	-0.120	3.02E-04	.995	.072	20.7	-0.132	3.30E-04	
		20	.996	.067	15.9	-0.100	2.49E-04	.996	.066	17.6	-0.110	2.74E-04	
		25	.995	.068	14.1	-0.086	2.13E-04	.996	.064	15.9	-0.100	2.48E-04	
		30	.995	.069	13.2	-0.083	2.08E-04	.996	.066	14.6	-0.093	2.32E-04	
	.3	5	.993	.083	31.2	-0.195	4.81E-04	.995	.069	34.3	-0.218	5.46E-04	
		10	.997	.055	21.3	-0.132	3.19E-04	.996	.062	23.3	-0.144	3.54E-04	
		15	.995	.073	17.6	-0.112	2.82E-04	.995	.072	19.7	-0.128	3.27E-04	
		20	.996	.066	14.9	-0.093	2.31E-04	.996	.062	16.6	-0.105	2.64E-04	
		25	.995	.068	13.1	-0.080	1.98E-04	.997	.059	14.5	-0.089	2.20E-04	
		30	.995	.069	12.3	-0.078	1.94E-04	.996	.067	13.6	-0.086	2.16E-04	

Table A17: Results of curve estimation for the CV (%) of the fixed slope: quadratic equations (model summary and parameter estimates, Model 2; the independent variable is number of sampled clusters) (contd.)

Case	ICC	Cluster size	Weight status										
			Unweighted					Weighted					
			Model summary		Parameter estimates			Model summary		Parameter estimates			
			R square	Sig.	Constant	b1	b2	R square	Sig.	Constant	b1	b2	
Covariance Case 2 (10 at within and 20 at between level)	.2	5	.994	.077	53.6	-0.335	8.25E-04	.995	.068	58.0	-0.355	8.65E-04	
		10	.997	.052	43.1	-0.265	6.39E-04	.997	.055	47.2	-0.285	6.81E-04	
		15	.995	.071	36.9	-0.236	5.96E-04	.995	.074	40.8	-0.261	6.59E-04	
		20	.996	.067	32.2	-0.205	5.13E-04	.996	.066	35.5	-0.226	5.68E-04	
		25	.995	.071	28.7	-0.178	4.42E-04	.996	.061	32.4	-0.206	5.16E-04	
		30	.996	.066	26.7	-0.168	4.17E-04	.996	.062	29.5	-0.187	4.66E-04	
	.3	5	.994	.076	54.3	-0.339	8.35E-04	.996	.066	60.0	-0.381	9.60E-04	
		10	.997	.052	41.9	-0.258	6.21E-04	.996	.060	45.5	-0.281	6.87E-04	
		15	.995	.071	35.3	-0.226	5.70E-04	.995	.073	39.1	-0.250	6.30E-04	
		20	.996	.067	30.5	-0.194	4.86E-04	.996	.067	34.0	-0.221	5.61E-04	
		25	.995	.071	27.0	-0.168	4.16E-04	.996	.062	30.0	-0.187	4.63E-04	
		30	.996	.066	25.1	-0.158	3.94E-04	.995	.069	27.8	-0.176	4.40E-04	
	.4	5	.994	.076	53.4	-0.333	8.21E-04	.994	.076	59.8	-0.390	1.00E-03	
		10	.997	.052	39.6	-0.244	5.89E-04	.997	.055	43.2	-0.264	6.42E-04	
		15	.995	.071	33.0	-0.212	5.33E-04	.997	.055	35.5	-0.216	5.29E-04	
		20	.996	.067	28.4	-0.180	4.52E-04	.996	.059	31.3	-0.199	5.03E-04	
		25	.995	.071	25.1	-0.155	3.85E-04	.996	.065	27.6	-0.172	4.29E-04	
		30	.996	.067	23.4	-0.147	3.67E-04	.996	.066	25.5	-0.158	3.91E-04	

Figure A25: CV (%) of the fixed slope: Model 2, Covariance Case 1 (20 at within and 10 at between level; graphical representation of first part of Table A17)

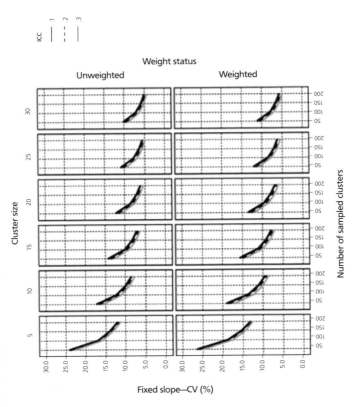

Figure A26: CV (%) of the fixed slope: Model 2, Covariance Case 2 (10 at within and 20 at between level; graphical representation of second part of Table A17)

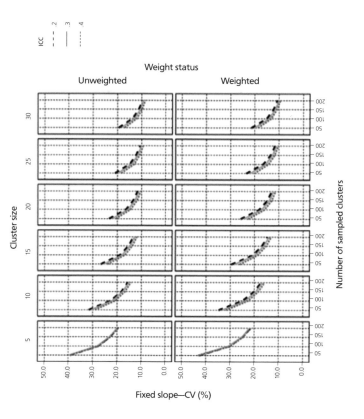

Table A18: Results of curve estimation for the CV (%) of the fixed slope: quadratic equations (model summary and parameter estimates, Model 3; the independent variable is cluster size)

Covariance structure	ICC	Number of sampled clusters	Weight status									
			Unweighted					Weighted				
			Model summary		Parameter estimates			Model summary		Parameter estimates		
			R square	Sig.	Constant	b1	b2	R square	Sig.	Constant	b1	b2
Covariance Case 1 (20 at within and 10 at between level)	.1	50	.978	.003	35.2	-1.902	0.036	.978	.003	38.4	-2.050	0.039
		100	.978	.003	25.0	-1.358	0.026	.978	.003	27.8	-1.512	0.029
		150	.971	.005	20.7	-1.138	0.022	.973	.004	22.6	-1.233	0.024
		200	.970	.005	17.6	-0.952	0.018	.973	.004	19.0	-1.012	0.019
	.2	50	.976	.004	33.4	-1.819	0.035	.977	.003	36.3	-1.947	0.037
		100	.978	.003	23.5	-1.277	0.024	.979	.003	25.9	-1.393	0.027
		150	.971	.005	19.4	-1.069	0.021	.975	.004	21.3	-1.159	0.022
		200	.971	.005	16.5	-0.893	0.017	.971	.005	18.1	-0.974	0.019
	.3	50	.976	.004	31.1	-1.699	0.033	.972	.005	34.0	-1.832	0.035
		100	.978	.003	21.9	-1.190	0.023	.975	.004	23.9	-1.291	0.025
		150	.971	.005	18.1	-0.997	0.019	.974	.004	19.7	-1.072	0.021
		200	.971	.005	15.3	-0.832	0.016	.972	.005	17.1	-0.928	0.018

Table A18: Results of curve estimation for the CV (%) of the fixed slope: quadratic equations (model summary and parameter estimates, Model 3; the independent variable is cluster size) (contd.)

Covariance structure	ICC	Number of sampled clusters	Weight status									
			Unweighted					Weighted				
			Model summary		Parameter estimates			Model summary		Parameter estimates		
			R square	Sig.	Constant	b1	b2	R square	Sig.	Constant	b1	b2
Covariance Case 2 (10 at within and 20 at between level)	.2	50	.982	.002	65.6	-3.413	0.064	.982	.002	70.7	-3.593	0.067
		100	.981	.003	47.9	-2.564	0.049	.981	.003	52.5	-2.795	0.053
		150	.974	.004	39.6	-2.153	0.041	.978	.003	43.3	-2.328	0.044
		200	.971	.005	33.9	-1.835	0.035	.972	.005	37.4	-2.013	0.039
	.3	50	.978	.003	63.5	-3.407	0.065	.974	.004	69.3	-3.689	0.070
		100	.980	.003	45.1	-2.436	0.046	.977	.004	49.2	-2.639	0.050
		150	.974	.004	37.1	-2.020	0.039	.976	.004	40.3	-2.162	0.041
		200	.971	.005	31.7	-1.708	0.033	.972	.005	35.2	-1.906	0.036
	.4	50	.977	.003	59.0	-3.186	0.061	.974	.004	65.3	-3.568	0.069
		100	.963	.007	41.5	-2.270	0.044	.980	.003	45.4	-2.420	0.046
		150	.973	.004	34.4	-1.877	0.036	.978	.003	37.3	-2.011	0.039
		200	.971	.005	29.3	-1.584	0.030	.972	.005	32.6	-1.765	0.034

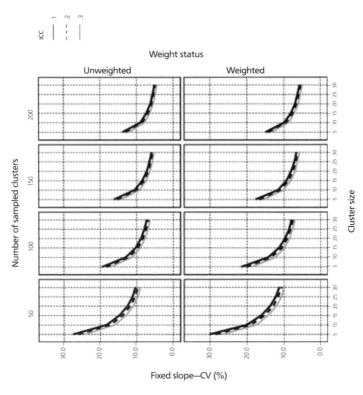

Figure A27: CV (%) of the fixed slope: Model 3, Covariance Case 1 (20 at within and 10 at between level; graphical representation of first part of Table A18)

Figure A28: CV (%) of the fixed slope: Model 3, Covariance Case 2 (10 at within and 20 at between level; graphical representation of second part of Table A18)

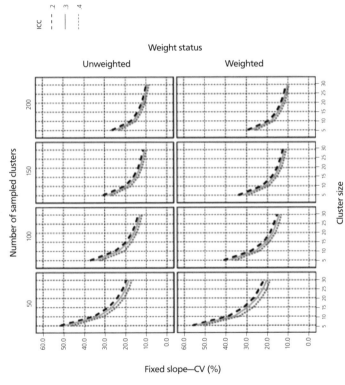

Table A19: Results of curve estimation for the CV (%) of the fixed slope: quadratic equations (model summary and parameter estimates, Model 3; the independent variable is number of sampled clusters)

Case	ICC	Cluster size	Weight status										
			Unweighted					Weighted					
			Model summary		Parameter estimates			Model summary		Parameter estimates			
			R square	Sig.	Constant	b1	b2	R square	Sig.	Constant	b1	b2
Covariance Case 1 (20 at within and 10 at between level)	.1	5	.994	.079	37.4	-0.229	5.61E-04	.996	.063	40.5	-0.240	5.66E-04
		10	.997	.054	24.9	-0.154	3.71E-04	.997	.054	27.4	-0.168	4.07E-04
		15	.995	.073	20.3	-0.130	3.26E-04	.995	.068	22.2	-0.140	3.47E-04
		20	.996	.066	17.1	-0.108	2.68E-04	.995	.069	18.8	-0.117	2.91E-04
		25	.995	.068	15.1	-0.093	2.29E-04	.994	.075	16.9	-0.109	2.78E-04
		30	.995	.068	14.1	-0.089	2.22E-04	.995	.071	15.4	-0.097	2.40E-04
	.2	5	.993	.082	35.6	-0.221	5.45E-04	.994	.075	38.7	-0.237	5.79E-04
		10	.997	.055	23.4	-0.144	3.49E-04	.997	.059	25.7	-0.156	3.72E-04
		15	.995	.073	19.1	-0.122	3.06E-04	.995	.073	21.0	-0.134	3.36E-04
		20	.996	.066	16.1	-0.101	2.51E-04	.996	.066	17.7	-0.111	2.77E-04
		25	.995	.068	14.1	-0.087	2.15E-04	.996	.064	16.0	-0.101	2.50E-04
		30	.995	.069	13.3	-0.084	2.09E-04	.996	.066	14.6	-0.093	2.33E-04
	.3	5	.993	.082	33.2	-0.206	5.08E-04	.995	.072	36.7	-0.233	5.86E-04
		10	.997	.055	21.8	-0.134	3.25E-04	.996	.060	23.7	-0.147	3.60E-04
		15	.995	.073	17.7	-0.113	2.85E-04	.995	.072	19.9	-0.129	3.29E-04
		20	.996	.066	14.9	-0.094	2.33E-04	.996	.062	16.7	-0.106	2.65E-04
		25	.995	.068	13.1	-0.081	1.99E-04	.997	.059	14.6	-0.090	2.21E-04
		30	.995	.069	12.4	-0.078	1.94E-04	.996	.066	13.6	-0.087	2.16E-04

Table A19: Results of curve estimation for the CV (%) of the fixed slope: quadratic equations (model summary and parameter estimates, Model 3; the independent variable is number of sampled clusters) (contd.)

Case	ICC	Cluster size	Weight status									
			Unweighted					Weighted				
			Model summary		Parameter estimates			Model summary		Parameter estimates		
			R square	Sig.	Constant	b1	b2	R square	Sig.	Constant	b1	b2
Covariance Case 2 (10 at within and 20 at between level)	.2	5	.995	.068	69.4	-0.412	9.95E-04	.997	.057	74.8	-0.433	1.04E-03
		10	.997	.050	48.2	-0.294	7.07E-04	.997	.054	52.6	-0.316	7.51E-04
		15	.995	.071	39.2	-0.251	6.32E-04	.995	.074	43.3	-0.277	6.98E-04
		20	.996	.067	33.4	-0.212	5.32E-04	.996	.066	36.8	-0.235	5.91E-04
		25	.995	.071	29.4	-0.183	4.54E-04	.996	.061	33.2	-0.212	5.30E-04
		30	.996	.066	27.1	-0.171	4.24E-04	.996	.062	30.0	-0.190	4.73E-04
	.3	5	.995	.074	67.8	-0.420	1.03E-03	.996	.063	75.0	-0.476	1.20E-03
		10	.997	.052	45.2	-0.278	6.71E-04	.996	.059	49.2	-0.303	7.41E-04
		15	.995	.071	36.7	-0.235	5.92E-04	.995	.072	40.6	-0.259	6.53E-04
		20	.996	.067	31.2	-0.198	4.97E-04	.996	.067	34.8	-0.226	5.74E-04
		25	.995	.071	27.4	-0.170	4.23E-04	.996	.061	30.5	-0.190	4.71E-04
		30	.996	.066	25.4	-0.160	3.98E-04	.995	.068	28.1	-0.178	4.44E-04
	.4	5	.994	.075	63.1	-0.393	9.70E-04	.995	.072	70.7	-0.460	1.18E-03
		10	.986	.117	42.7	-0.284	7.37E-04	.997	.056	45.6	-0.280	6.80E-04
		15	.995	.071	33.9	-0.217	5.47E-04	.997	.055	36.4	-0.222	5.43E-04
		20	.996	.067	28.8	-0.183	4.58E-04	.996	.059	31.7	-0.202	5.10E-04
		25	.995	.071	25.3	-0.157	3.90E-04	.996	.065	27.9	-0.174	4.34E-04
		30	.996	.066	23.5	-0.148	3.69E-04	.996	.065	25.7	-0.159	3.94E-04

Figure A29: CV (%) of the fixed slope: Model 3, Covariance Case 1 (20 at within and 10 at between level; graphical representation of first part of Table A19)

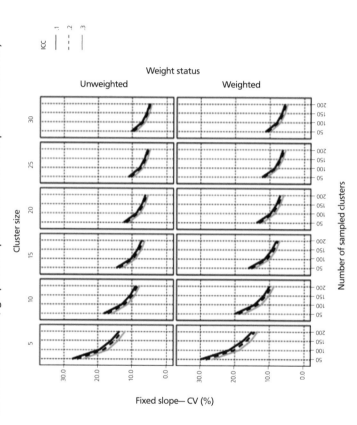

Figure A30: CV (%) of the fixed slope: Model 3, Covariance Case 2 (10 at within and 20 at between level; graphical representation of second part of Table A19)

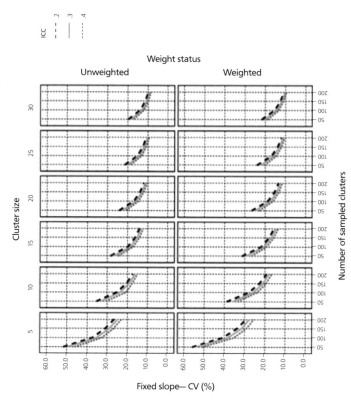

Table A20: Results of curve estimation for the CV (%) of the slope of random intercepts: quadratic equations (model summary and parameter estimates, Model 3; the independent variable is cluster size)

Covariance structure	ICC	Number of sampled clusters	Weight status										
			Unweighted					Weighted					
			Model summary		Parameter estimates			Model summary		Parameter estimates			
			R square	Sig.	Constant	b1	b2	R square	Sig.	Constant	b1	b2	
Covariance Case 1 (20 at within and 10 at between level)	.1	50	.960	.008	62.7	-3.020	0.061	.957	.009	69.8	-3.381	0.068	
		100	.959	.008	42.0	-1.972	0.040	.956	.009	46.1	-2.151	0.044	
		150	.968	.006	33.6	-1.538	0.031	.968	.006	37.4	-1.726	0.034	
		200	.965	.007	28.9	-1.317	0.026	.964	.007	32.3	-1.518	0.031	
	.2	50	.955	.009	69.8	-2.753	0.057	.953	.010	77.2	-3.088	0.064	
		100	.956	.009	45.9	-1.699	0.035	.954	.010	50.7	-1.882	0.039	
		150	.965	.007	36.4	-1.286	0.026	.962	.007	40.5	-1.434	0.029	
		200	.958	.009	31.4	-1.108	0.022	.962	.007	34.9	-1.236	0.025	
	.3	50	.954	.010	75.6	-2.535	0.052	.959	.008	86.3	-3.133	0.065	
		100	.954	.010	49.9	-1.567	0.032	.942	.014	55.4	-1.752	0.036	
		150	.960	.008	39.6	-1.166	0.024	.954	.010	44.4	-1.375	0.028	
		200	.951	.011	34.0	-0.986	0.020	.950	.011	37.7	-1.114	0.023	

Table A20: Results of curve estimation for the CV (%) of the slope of random intercepts: quadratic equations (model summary and parameter estimates, Model 3; the independent variable is cluster size) (contd.)

Covariance structure	ICC	Number of sampled clusters	Weight status										
			Unweighted					Weighted					
			Model summary		Parameter estimates			Model summary		Parameter estimates			
			R square	Sig.	Constant	b1	b2	R square	Sig.	Constant	b1	b2	
Covariance Case 2 (10 at within and 20 at between level)	.2	50	.965	.007	32.8	-1.570	0.031	.959	.008	35.7	-1.689	0.034	
		100	.958	.009	22.8	-1.100	0.022	.958	.009	25.1	-1.212	0.024	
		150	.968	.006	18.6	-0.894	0.018	.967	.006	20.5	-0.979	0.019	
		200	.965	.007	16.0	-0.778	0.016	.965	.007	17.7	-0.862	0.017	
	.3	50	.950	.011	36.7	-1.486	0.030	.956	.009	40.9	-1.696	0.035	
		100	.946	.012	24.5	-0.961	0.020	.950	.011	27.2	-1.071	0.022	
		150	.964	.007	19.6	-0.732	0.015	.962	.008	21.6	-0.799	0.016	
		200	.960	.008	17.0	-0.656	0.013	.954	.010	18.9	-0.728	0.015	
	.4	50	.946	.012	39.8	-1.411	0.029	.945	.013	43.9	-1.589	0.033	
		100	.944	.013	26.1	-0.859	0.018	.947	.012	29.4	-0.999	0.020	
		150	.961	.008	20.8	-0.635	0.013	.960	.008	23.3	-0.752	0.015	
		200	.955	.010	18.1	-0.582	0.012	.950	.011	20.0	-0.649	0.013	

Figure A31: CV (%) of the slope of random intercepts: Model 3, Covariance Case 1 (20 at within and 10 at between level; graphical representation of first part of Table A20)

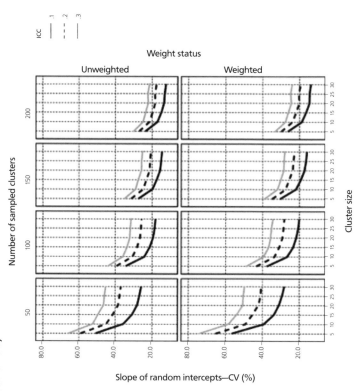

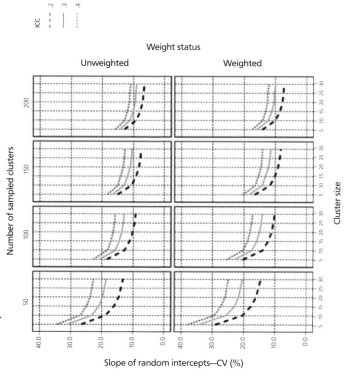

Figure A32: CV (%) of the slope of random intercepts: Model 3, Covariance Case 2 (10 at within and 20 at between level; graphical representation of second part of Table A20)

Table A21: Results of curve estimation for the CV (%) of the slope of random intercepts: quadratic equations (model summary and parameter estimates, Model 3; the independent variable is number of sampled clusters)

Covariance structure	ICC	Cluster size	Weight status										
			Unweighted					Weighted					
			Model summary		Parameter estimates			Model summary		Parameter estimates			
			R square	Sig.	Constant	b1	b2	R square	Sig.	Constant	b1	b2	
Covariance Case 1 (20 at within and 10 at between level)	.1	5	.995	.071	72.1	-0.495	1.27E-03	.993	.083	80.7	-0.563	1.47E-03	
		10	.993	.082	50.0	-0.336	8.66E-04	.993	.084	55.2	-0.371	9.52E-04	
		15	.994	.079	42.8	-0.278	7.00E-04	.993	.083	47.0	-0.305	7.69E-04	
		20	.996	.060	39.2	-0.257	6.44E-04	.997	.057	43.3	-0.279	6.83E-04	
		25	.996	.065	37.8	-0.252	6.50E-04	.998	.045	41.3	-0.273	7.01E-04	
		30	.996	.063	36.0	-0.232	5.74E-04	.998	.044	38.9	-0.246	6.08E-04	
	.2	5	.994	.075	84.6	-0.596	1.55E-03	.993	.082	93.2	-0.652	1.69E-03	
		10	.994	.077	63.1	-0.423	1.08E-03	.994	.077	68.9	-0.461	1.19E-03	
		15	.993	.086	57.6	-0.381	9.67E-04	.991	.092	63.2	-0.416	1.05E-03	
		20	.996	.061	53.4	-0.349	8.71E-04	.995	.069	58.7	-0.381	9.47E-04	
		25	.996	.064	52.4	-0.344	8.73E-04	.996	.060	57.1	-0.374	9.54E-04	
		30	.996	.063	51.1	-0.329	8.09E-04	.996	.067	56.8	-0.372	9.32E-04	
	.3	5	.994	.074	93.9	-0.657	1.70E-03	.993	.084	106.3	-0.755	1.96E-03	
		10	.994	.074	73.8	-0.495	1.27E-03	.995	.074	82.6	-0.565	1.46E-03	
		15	.992	.088	69.4	-0.464	1.18E-03	.992	.087	75.7	-0.507	1.31E-03	
		20	.996	.063	64.5	-0.421	1.05E-03	.997	.051	69.8	-0.442	1.08E-03	
		25	.996	.064	63.8	-0.418	1.06E-03	.997	.056	70.1	-0.457	1.16E-03	
		30	.996	.066	62.5	-0.400	9.82E-04	.994	.074	69.0	-0.448	1.12E-03	

Table A21: Results of curve estimation for the CV (%) of the slope of random intercepts: quadratic equations (model summary and parameter estimates, Model 3; the independent variable is number of sampled clusters) (contd.)

Covariance structure	ICC	Cluster size	Weight status										
			Unweighted					Weighted					
			Model summary		Parameter estimates			Model summary		Parameter estimates			
			R square	Sig.	Constant	b1	b2	R square	Sig.	Constant	b1	b2	
Covariance Case 2 (10 at within and 20 at between level)	.2	5	.995	.071	37.1	-0.242	6.12E-04	.995	.071	40.1	-0.256	6.38E-04	
		10	.992	.089	26.3	-0.176	4.53E-04	.992	.090	28.1	-0.181	4.58E-04	
		15	.994	.080	22.4	-0.145	3.64E-04	.993	.086	24.6	-0.159	3.95E-04	
		20	.995	.069	20.3	-0.132	3.31E-04	.993	.083	22.2	-0.144	3.61E-04	
		25	.996	.062	19.6	-0.132	3.39E-04	.996	.065	21.5	-0.144	3.70E-04	
		30	.995	.070	18.3	-0.118	2.97E-04	.995	.073	20.2	-0.132	3.36E-04	
	.3	5	.995	.072	44.0	-0.304	7.86E-04	.996	.066	48.7	-0.337	8.73E-04	
		10	.992	.091	32.6	-0.220	5.69E-04	.993	.081	36.2	-0.245	6.31E-04	
		15	.993	.085	29.0	-0.187	4.67E-04	.992	.090	31.5	-0.200	4.97E-04	
		20	.995	.070	27.5	-0.179	4.48E-04	.996	.064	30.0	-0.194	4.82E-04	
		25	.995	.067	27.0	-0.182	4.69E-04	.996	.066	29.6	-0.201	5.25E-04	
		30	.996	.062	25.7	-0.166	4.12E-04	.995	.069	28.5	-0.188	4.79E-04	
	.4	5	.994	.077	49.3	-0.348	9.12E-04	.996	.064	53.7	-0.368	9.41E-04	
		10	.992	.088	37.8	-0.256	6.61E-04	.995	.071	41.0	-0.270	6.83E-04	
		15	.992	.091	34.6	-0.225	5.64E-04	.993	.086	37.9	-0.246	6.17E-04	
		20	.995	.069	33.1	-0.215	5.37E-04	.996	.064	35.8	-0.230	5.70E-04	
		25	.995	.069	32.6	-0.218	5.60E-04	.995	.069	35.7	-0.238	6.15E-04	
		30	.996	.062	31.5	-0.203	5.03E-04	.992	.088	34.4	-0.223	5.60E-04	

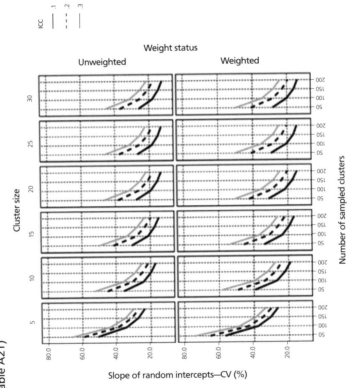

Figure A33: CV (%) of the slope of random intercepts: Model 3, Covariance Case 1 (20 at within and 10 at between level; graphical representation of first part of Table A21)

Figure A34: CV (%) of the slope of random intercepts: Model 3, Covariance Case 2 (10 at within and 20 at between level; graphical representation of second part of Table A21)

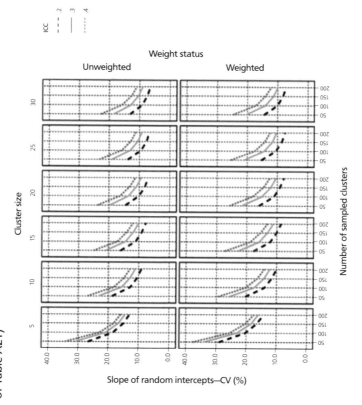

Table A22: Results of curve estimation for the CV (%) of the slope of random intercepts: quadratic equations (model summary and parameter estimates, Model 4; the independent variable is cluster size)

Covariance structure	ICC	Number of sampled clusters	Weight status									
			Unweighted					Weighted				
			Model summary		Parameter estimates			Model summary		Parameter estimates		
			R square	Sig.	Constant	b1	b2	R square	Sig.	Constant	b1	b2
Covariance Case 1 (20 at within and 10 at between level)	.1	50	.930	.019	271.6	-6.54	0.112	.956	.009	285.1	-6.26	0.104
		100	.986	.002	256.1	-10.32	0.202	.995	.000	258.1	-9.30	0.180
		150	.988	.001	223.2	-9.55	0.186	.987	.001	244.5	-10.32	0.198
		200	.978	.003	207.8	-9.45	0.186	.989	.001	224.2	-10.01	0.197
	.2	50	.860	.052	325.1	-6.30	0.113	.619	.235	343.6	-6.95	0.145
		100	.956	.009	285.3	-9.89	0.205	.953	.010	299.6	-9.59	0.195
		150	.946	.013	243.1	-8.83	0.182	.972	.005	257.6	-8.29	0.162
		200	.963	.007	214.0	-7.75	0.157	.960	.008	240.0	-8.73	0.175
	.3	50	.592	.260	355.1	-4.06	0.058	.495	.359	384.2	-4.61	0.085
		100	.905	.029	307.6	-9.11	0.193	.914	.025	336.1	-9.62	0.202
		150	.935	.017	254.9	-7.64	0.166	.950	.011	293.9	-9.76	0.213
		200	.914	.025	228.7	-7.36	0.161	.923	.021	247.8	-7.67	0.169

Table A22: Results of curve estimation for the CV (%) of the slope of random intercepts: quadratic equations (model summary and parameter estimates, Model 4; the independent variable is cluster size) (contd.)

Covariance structure	ICC	Number of sampled clusters	Weight status										
			Unweighted					Weighted					
			Model summary		Parameter estimates			Model summary		Parameter estimates			
			R square	Sig.	Constant	b1	b2	R square	Sig.	Constant	b1	b2	
Covariance Case 2 (10 at within and 20 at between level)	.2	50	.965	.006	46.4	-2.26	0.044	.965	.007	50.4	-2.43	0.048	
		100	.958	.008	34.1	-1.76	0.035	.959	.008	36.7	-1.85	0.037	
		150	.964	.007	27.9	-1.45	0.029	.964	.007	30.7	-1.58	0.031	
		200	.962	.007	24.3	-1.26	0.025	.961	.008	26.6	-1.38	0.028	
	.3	50	.955	.010	51.4	-2.23	0.045	.956	.009	56.2	-2.45	0.050	
		100	.950	.011	35.3	-1.53	0.031	.956	.009	38.8	-1.67	0.033	
		150	.960	.008	28.3	-1.19	0.024	.965	.007	31.3	-1.32	0.026	
		200	.959	.008	24.9	-1.09	0.022	.959	.008	27.6	-1.21	0.024	
	.4	50	.947	.012	54.1	-2.07	0.042	.947	.012	59.2	-2.29	0.047	
		100	.949	.011	36.2	-1.33	0.027	.953	.010	40.7	-1.54	0.031	
		150	.964	.007	29.2	-1.04	0.021	.964	.007	32.6	-1.21	0.025	
		200	.959	.008	25.6	-0.96	0.020	.956	.009	28.2	-1.06	0.022	

Figure A35: CV (%) of the slope of random intercepts: Model 4, Covariance Case 1 (20 at within and 10 at between level; graphical representation of first part of Table A22)

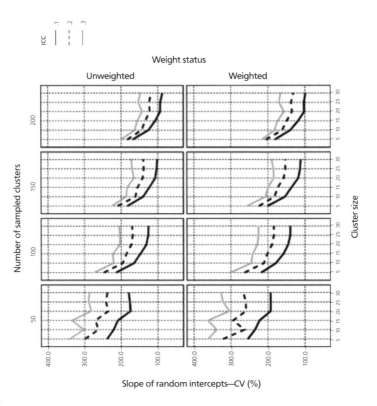

Figure A36: CV (%) of the slope of random intercepts: Model 4, Covariance Case 2 (10 at within and 20 at between level; graphical representation of second part of Table A22)

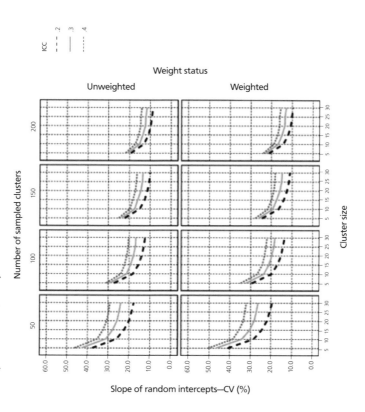

Table A23: Results of curve estimation for the CV (%) of the slope of random intercepts: quadratic equations (model summary and parameter estimates, Model 4; the independent variable is number of sampled clusters)

Covariance structure	ICC	Cluster size	Weight status									
			Unweighted					Weighted				
			Model summary		Parameter estimates			Model summary		Parameter estimates		
			R square	Sig.	Constant	b1	b2	R square	Sig.	Constant	b1	b2
Covariance Case 1 (20 at within and 10 at between level)	.1	5	.993	.086	273.7	-0.743	1.07E-03	.992	.091	292.2	-0.866	1.59E-03
		10	.997	.055	289.6	-1.606	3.95E-03	.997	.058	305.6	-1.645	4.11E-03
		15	.994	.075	285.0	-1.773	4.45E-03	.988	.108	300.0	-1.816	4.59E-03
		20	.999	.029	231.3	-1.283	2.99E-03	.999	.026	253.9	-1.380	3.11E-03
		25	.998	.050	243.5	-1.549	4.01E-03	.999	.033	264.7	-1.666	4.29E-03
		30	.996	.065	248.5	-1.594	3.97E-03	.999	.032	264.7	-1.645	4.09E-03
	.2	5	1.000	.008	364.3	-1.439	2.67E-03	1.000	.003	400.8	-1.787	4.05E-03
		10	.998	.040	351.7	-2.042	5.05E-03	.998	.044	326.6	-1.441	3.10E-03
		15	.990	.099	376.2	-2.473	6.38E-03	.985	.121	404.7	-2.613	6.76E-03
		20	.998	.050	312.4	-1.791	4.22E-03	.996	.067	345.5	-1.994	4.75E-03
		25	.996	.067	334.9	-2.182	5.65E-03	.995	.069	357.1	-2.281	5.95E-03
		30	.996	.065	320.9	-1.927	4.63E-03	.991	.092	366.7	-2.353	5.94E-03
	.3	5	1.000	.016	429.6	-1.994	4.22E-03	1.000	.020	432.2	-1.523	2.23E-03
		10	.994	.078	405.4	-2.386	5.93E-03	.994	.079	456.4	-2.753	6.97E-03
		15	.989	.105	473.8	-3.277	8.53E-03	.990	.101	514.6	-3.586	9.50E-03
		20	.997	.054	381.8	-2.304	5.58E-03	.999	.032	400.2	-2.173	4.79E-03
		25	.993	.083	400.2	-2.604	6.90E-03	.996	.060	450.0	-3.009	8.09E-03
		30	.992	.090	387.7	-2.330	5.70E-03	.990	.101	453.2	-2.967	7.72E-03

Table A23: Results of curve estimation for the CV (%) of the slope of random intercepts: quadratic equations (model summary and parameter estimates, Model 4; the independent variable is number of sampled clusters) (contd.)

Covariance structure	ICC	Cluster size	Weight status										
			Unweighted					Weighted					
			Model summary		Parameter estimates			Model summary		Parameter estimates			
			R square	Sig.	Constant	b1	b2	R square	Sig.	Constant	b1	b2
Covariance Case 2 (10 at within and 20 at between level)	.2	5	.998	.049	50.7	-0.303	7.32E-04	.995	.071	55.2	-0.332	8.16E-04
		10	.995	.070	35.9	-0.230	5.82E-04	.993	.084	39.3	-0.252	6.37E-04
		15	.994	.075	31.2	-0.204	5.16E-04	.994	.079	33.8	-0.216	5.40E-04
		20	.996	.065	27.6	-0.177	4.41E-04	.994	.078	30.3	-0.197	4.95E-04
		25	.997	.053	26.3	-0.176	4.56E-04	.997	.056	28.9	-0.192	4.95E-04
		30	.995	.070	24.5	-0.159	3.99E-04	.994	.075	26.8	-0.174	4.39E-04
	.3	5	.996	.064	60.0	-0.402	1.03E-03	.996	.064	65.3	-0.433	1.11E-03
		10	.994	.080	43.7	-0.293	7.56E-04	.995	.073	47.4	-0.310	7.90E-04
		15	.993	.086	38.5	-0.247	6.18E-04	.992	.089	41.8	-0.267	6.69E-04
		20	.996	.064	35.8	-0.232	5.76E-04	.997	.059	39.0	-0.250	6.17E-04
		25	.996	.063	35.0	-0.238	6.17E-04	.996	.062	38.4	-0.263	6.91E-04
		30	.996	.060	33.3	-0.217	5.42E-04	.995	.070	36.9	-0.245	6.26E-04
	.4	5	.994	.077	65.6	-0.455	1.19E-03	.996	.062	70.8	-0.471	1.19E-03
		10	.993	.084	49.3	-0.330	8.50E-04	.995	.068	53.2	-0.343	8.61E-04
		15	.992	.091	45.0	-0.293	7.37E-04	.993	.085	49.3	-0.322	8.09E-04
		20	.995	.068	42.8	-0.280	6.99E-04	.996	.062	46.3	-0.298	7.39E-04
		25	.996	.066	41.9	-0.281	7.23E-04	.995	.069	45.8	-0.307	7.95E-04
		30	.996	.061	40.6	-0.264	6.59E-04	.993	.083	44.5	-0.291	7.35E-04

Figure A37: CV (%) of the slope of random intercepts: Model 4, Covariance Case 1 (20 at within and 10 at between level; graphical representation of first part of Table A23)

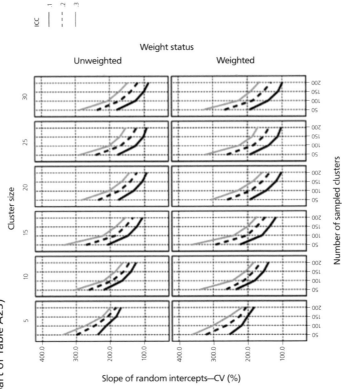

Figure A38: CV (%) of the slope of random intercepts: Model 4, Covariance Case 2 (10 at within and 20 at between level; graphical representation of second part of Table A23)

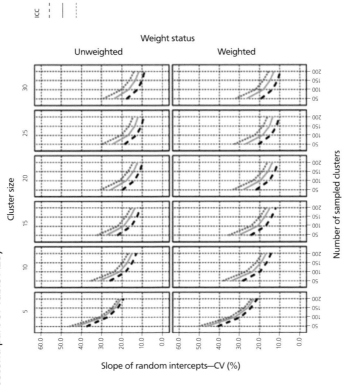

Table A24: Results of curve estimation for the CV (%) of the mean of random slopes: quadratic equations (model summary and parameter estimates, Model 4; the independent variable is cluster size)

Covariance structure	ICC	Number of sampled clusters	Weight status										
			Unweighted					Weighted					
			Model summary		Parameter estimates			Model summary		Parameter estimates			
			R square	Sig.	Constant	b1	b2	R square	Sig.	Constant	b1	b2	
Covariance Case 1 (20 at within and 10 at between level)	.1	50	.962	.007	47.6	-2.97	0.059	.960	.008	52.0	-3.25	0.065	
		100	.965	.006	31.5	-1.92	0.038	.964	.007	34.7	-2.12	0.042	
		150	.966	.006	24.9	-1.48	0.029	.966	.006	26.7	-1.57	0.031	
		200	.963	.007	20.8	-1.22	0.024	.970	.005	21.9	-1.25	0.024	
	.2	50	.965	.006	42.3	-2.60	0.052	.933	.017	45.3	-2.81	0.057	
		100	.967	.006	28.3	-1.69	0.034	.972	.005	30.7	-1.81	0.036	
		150	.967	.006	22.9	-1.35	0.027	.969	.006	24.5	-1.42	0.028	
		200	.965	.007	18.9	-1.08	0.021	.967	.006	20.4	-1.16	0.023	
	.3	50	.963	.007	38.0	-2.30	0.046	.960	.008	41.2	-2.46	0.049	
		100	.967	.006	25.3	-1.46	0.029	.963	.007	27.4	-1.58	0.031	
		150	.959	.008	20.8	-1.21	0.024	.959	.008	22.3	-1.28	0.025	
		200	.961	.008	17.4	-0.99	0.019	.962	.007	19.0	-1.08	0.021	

Table A24: Results of curve estimation for the CV (%) of the mean of random slopes: quadratic equations (model summary and parameter estimates, Model 4; the independent variable is cluster size) (contd.)

Covariance structure	ICC	Number of sampled clusters	Weight status										
			Unweighted					Weighted					
			Model summary		Parameter estimates			Model summary		Parameter estimates			
			R square	Sig.	Constant	b1	b2	R square	Sig.	Constant	b1	b2	
Covariance Case 2 (10 at within and 20 at between level)	.2	50	.969	.005	80.7	-4.72	0.094	.970	.005	86.6	-4.96	0.097	
		100	.970	.005	55.1	-3.20	0.064	.971	.005	61.6	-3.58	0.072	
		150	.963	.007	44.6	-2.58	0.052	.965	.007	49.9	-2.89	0.058	
		200	.963	.007	37.6	-2.14	0.043	.963	.007	41.8	-2.37	0.047	
	.3	50	.968	.006	71.9	-4.08	0.078	.966	.006	79.0	-4.47	0.086	
		100	.972	.005	50.0	-2.75	0.052	.968	.006	54.7	-3.02	0.057	
		150	.964	.007	40.3	-2.20	0.041	.966	.006	43.7	-2.36	0.044	
		200	.952	.010	34.1	-1.81	0.034	.958	.009	37.9	-2.03	0.038	
	.4	50	.973	.004	66.3	-3.83	0.074	.972	.005	71.9	-4.14	0.081	
		100	.981	.003	45.8	-2.58	0.049	.982	.002	49.4	-2.73	0.052	
		150	.980	.003	37.5	-2.12	0.041	.982	.002	40.5	-2.26	0.043	
		200	.978	.003	31.9	-1.78	0.034	.979	.003	34.9	-1.94	0.037	

Figure A39: CV (%) of the mean of random slopes: Model 4, Covariance Case 1 (20 at within and 10 at between level; graphical representation of first part of Table A24)

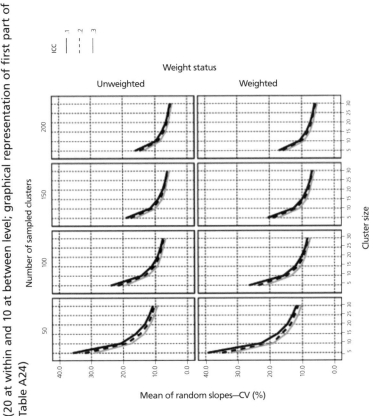

Figure A40: CV (%) of the mean of random slopes: Model 4, Covariance Case 2 (10 at within and 20 at between level; graphical representation of second part of Table A24)

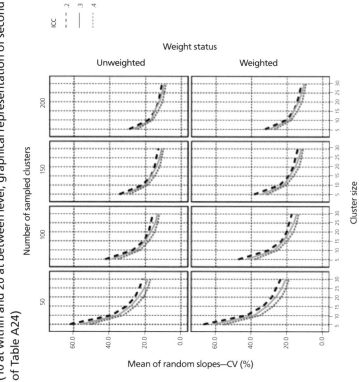

Table A25: Results of curve estimation for the CV (%) of the mean of random slopes: quadratic equations (model summary and parameter estimates, Model 4; the independent variable is number of sampled clusters)

Covariance structure	ICC	Cluster size	Unweighted					Weighted				
			Model summary		Parameter estimates			Model summary		Parameter estimates		
			R square	Sig.	Constant	b1	b2	R square	Sig.	Constant	b1	b2
Covariance Case 1 (20 at within and 10 at between level)	.1	5	.994	.074	51.2	-0.354	9.00E-04	.996	.061	55.8	-0.382	9.44E-04
		10	.995	.069	29.0	-0.189	4.67E-04	.996	.062	31.5	-0.205	5.09E-04
		15	.994	.075	22.6	-0.150	3.86E-04	.995	.071	24.5	-0.160	4.06E-04
		20	.996	.066	18.3	-0.117	2.92E-04	.995	.073	20.0	-0.126	3.11E-04
		25	.996	.060	16.3	-0.103	2.57E-04	.994	.074	18.0	-0.117	2.99E-04
		30	.996	.063	14.8	-0.092	2.28E-04	.996	.065	16.1	-0.101	2.51E-04
	.2	5	.992	.087	44.8	-0.298	7.44E-04	.993	.081	49.2	-0.334	8.42E-04
		10	.994	.075	26.2	-0.166	4.06E-04	1.000	.006	24.5	-0.122	2.45E-04
		15	.995	.072	20.2	-0.129	3.24E-04	.994	.078	22.5	-0.146	3.71E-04
		20	.995	.067	16.8	-0.104	2.54E-04	.996	.063	18.5	-0.115	2.85E-04
		25	.997	.058	15.1	-0.094	2.33E-04	.996	.060	16.9	-0.106	2.60E-04
		30	.996	.062	14.2	-0.089	2.18E-04	.997	.058	15.5	-0.097	2.37E-04
	.3	5	.989	.104	40.7	-0.275	6.99E-04	.992	.088	44.6	-0.305	7.88E-04
		10	.997	.054	23.9	-0.149	3.59E-04	.997	.055	26.0	-0.165	4.08E-04
		15	.993	.086	18.6	-0.119	3.01E-04	.994	.078	20.6	-0.134	3.41E-04
		20	.995	.069	15.7	-0.094	2.26E-04	.996	.067	17.4	-0.106	2.60E-04
		25	.997	.058	13.6	-0.076	1.74E-04	.997	.053	14.9	-0.084	1.91E-04
		30	.995	.067	12.5	-0.073	1.69E-04	.996	.064	13.8	-0.081	1.90E-04

Table A25: Results of curve estimation for the CV (%) of the mean of random slopes: quadratic equations (model summary and parameter estimates, Model 4; the independent variable is number of sampled clusters) (contd.)

Covariance structure	ICC	Cluster size	Weight status									
			Unweighted					Weighted				
			Model summary		Parameter estimates			Model summary		Parameter estimates		
			R square	Sig.	Constant	b1	b2	R square	Sig.	Constant	b1	b2
Covariance Case 2 (10 at within and 20 at between level)	.2	5	.993	.083	86.4	-0.570	1.43E-03	.995	.069	91.1	-0.561	1.35E-03
		10	.996	.061	53.4	-0.340	8.29E-04	.997	.052	58.1	-0.358	8.56E-04
		15	.995	.070	42.0	-0.275	6.95E-04	.994	.078	46.2	-0.299	7.51E-04
		20	.995	.072	35.3	-0.221	5.46E-04	.996	.064	38.8	-0.243	6.06E-04
		25	.996	.062	30.9	-0.175	4.01E-04	.997	.059	35.0	-0.209	4.97E-04
		30	.999	.037	28.6	-0.162	3.67E-04	.998	.044	31.4	-0.182	4.23E-04
	.3	5	.995	.071	77.0	-0.491	1.22E-03	.997	.059	85.6	-0.561	1.43E-03
		10	.997	.053	47.6	-0.292	6.93E-04	.996	.061	52.5	-0.329	8.10E-04
		15	.995	.069	38.0	-0.231	5.82E-04	.995	.074	42.2	-0.262	6.68E-04
		20	.996	.060	32.4	-0.200	5.02E-04	.996	.060	35.9	-0.226	5.73E-04
		25	.994	.074	28.2	-0.181	4.65E-04	.995	.068	31.3	-0.199	5.07E-04
		30	.995	.070	25.6	-0.162	4.12E-04	.995	.071	28.4	-0.182	4.63E-04
	.4	5	.993	.081	70.7	-0.459	1.16E-03	.994	.079	77.1	-0.508	1.30E-03
		10	.997	.059	43.4	-0.262	6.29E-04	.997	.058	47.0	-0.280	6.74E-04
		15	.996	.065	34.9	-0.219	5.47E-04	.997	.052	37.3	-0.223	5.39E-04
		20	.996	.065	28.9	-0.184	4.63E-04	.997	.056	31.8	-0.205	5.18E-04
		25	.995	.072	25.3	-0.157	3.90E-04	.995	.068	27.9	-0.176	4.43E-04
		30	.996	.065	23.4	-0.147	3.66E-04	.996	.066	25.6	-0.159	3.95E-04

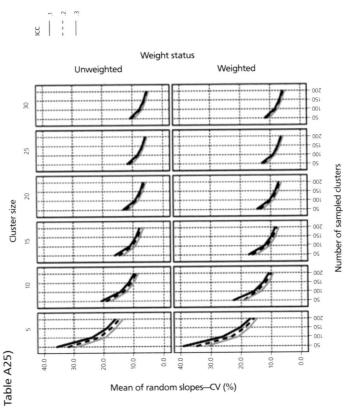

Figure A41: CV (%) of the mean of random slopes: Model 4, Covariance Case 1 (20 at within and 10 at between level; graphical representation of first part of Table A25)

Figure A42: CV (%) of the mean of random slopes: Model 4, Covariance Case 2 (10 at within and 20 at between level; graphical representation of second part of Table A25)

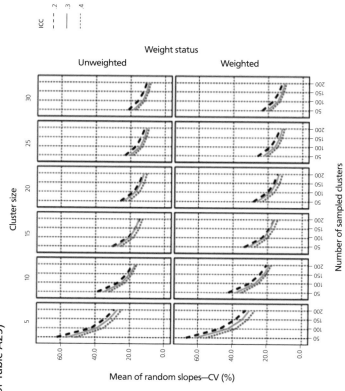

References

Afshartous, D. (1995). Determination of sample size for multilevel model design. In V. S. Williams, L. V. Jones, & I. Olkin (Eds.), *Perspectives on statistics for educational research: Proceedings of the National Institute for Statistical Sciences* (NISS), Technical Report #35 (pp. 20–22). Triangle Park, NC: National Institute of Statistical Sciences.

Aitkin, M., Anderson, D., & Hinde, J. (1981). Statistical modelling of data on teaching styles. *Journal of the Royal Statistical Society, Series A, 144*(4), 419–461.

Aitkin, M., & Longford, N. (1986). Statistical modelling issues in school effectiveness studies. *Journal of the Royal Statistical Society, Series A, 149*(1), 1–43.

Anderson, J. O., Milford, T., & Ross, S. P. (2009). Multilevel modeling with HLM: Taking a second look at PISA. In M. C. Shelley, L. D. Yore, & B. Hand (Eds.), *Quality research in literacy and science education* (pp. 263–286). Dordrecht, the Netherlands: Springer Science + Business Media B. V.

Asparouhov, T., & Muthén, B. (2006). *Multilevel modeling of complex survey data: ASA Section on Survey Research Methods, 2718–2726*. Retrieved from http://www.statmodel.com/download/SurveyJSM1.pdf

Asparouhov, T., Muthén, B., & Muthén, L. (2006). General multi-level modeling with sampling weights. *Communications in Statistics: Theory and Methods, 35*(3), 439–460.

Baker, D. P., Goesling, B., & Letendre, G. K. (2002). Socioeconomic status, school quality, and national economic development: A cross-national analysis of the "Heyneman-Loxley effect" on mathematics and science achievement. *Comparative Education Review, 46*(3), 291–312.

Bell, B. A., Morgan, G. B., Schoeneberger, J. A., Loudermilk, B. L., Kromrey, J. D., & Ferron, J. M. (2010). *Dancing the sample size limbo with mixed models: How low can you go?* (SAS Global Forum 2010 Posters Paper 197-2010). Retrieved from http://support.sas.com/resources/papers/proceedings10/197-2010.pdf

Braun, H., Jenkins, F., & Grigg, W. (2006). *Comparing private schools and public schools using hierarchical linear modeling* (NCES 2006-461). Washington, DC: U.S. Government Printing Office.

Brown, P., & Lauder, H. (1996). Education, globalization and economic development. *Journal of Education Policy, 11*(1), 1–25.

Bryk, A. S., & Raudenbush, S. W. (1992). *Hierarchical linear models: Applications and data analysis methods*, Thousand Oaks, CA: Sage.

Burstein, L. (1980). The analysis of multi-level data in educational research and evaluation. *Review of Research in Education*, *8*, 158–233.

Caro, D. H. (2010). *Measuring family socioeconomic status: A methodological proposal for PIRLS*. Manuscript submitted for publication.

Caro, D. H., & Lehmann, R. (2009). Achievement inequalities in Hamburg schools: How do they change as students get older? *School Effectiveness and School Improvement*, *20*(4), 407–431.

Caro, D. H., McDonald, T., & Willms, J. D. (2009). Socio-economic status and academic achievement trajectories from childhood to adolescence. *Canadian Journal of Education*, *32*(3), 558–590.

Chantala, K., Blanchette, D., & Suchindran, C. M. (2006). *Software to compute sampling weights for multilevel analysis*. Chapel Hill, NC: Carolina Population Center, University of North Carolina. Retrieved from http://www.cpc.unc.edu/restools/data_analysis/ml_sampling_weights

Cheong, Y. F., Fotiu, R. P., & Raudenbush, S.W. (2001). Efficiency and robustness of alternative estimators for two- and three-level models: The cases of NAEP. *Journal of Educational and Behavioral Statistics*, *26*(4), 411–429.

Cochran, W. G. (1977). *Sampling techniques* (3rd ed.). New York, NY: Wiley.

Cohen, J. (1988). *Statistical power analysis for the behavioral sciences* (2nd ed.). Hillsdale, NJ: Lawrence Erlbaum.

Cohen, J. (1998). Determining sample sizes for surveys with data analyzed by hierarchical linear models. *Journal of Official Statistics*, *14*(3), 267–275.

Cronbach, L. J. (1967). How can instruction be adapted to individual differences? In R. M. Gagné (Ed.), *Learning and individual differences*. Columbus, OH: Merrill Books.

Dale, R. (2000). Globalization and education: Demonstrating a "common world educational culture" or locating a "globally structured educational agenda"? *Educational Theory*, *50*(4), 427–448.

Decker, P. T., Rice, J. K., & Moore, M. T. (1997). *Education and the economy: An indicators report* (NCES 97-269). Washington, DC: U.S. Government Printing Office.

De Leeuw, J., & Kreft, I. (1986). Random coefficient models for multilevel analysis. *Journal of Educational Statistics*, *11*(1), 57–85.

Desimone, L. M., Smith, T., Baker, D., & Ueno, K. (2005). Assessing barriers to the reform of U.S. mathematics instruction from an international perspective. *American Educational Research Journal*, *42*(3), 501–535.

Foy, P., & Olson, J. F. (Eds.). (2009). *TIMSS 2007 international database and user guide*. Chestnut Hill, MA: Boston College.

Goldstein, H. (1986). Multilevel mixed linear model analysis using iterative generalized least squares. *Biometrika*, *73*(1), 43–56.

Goldstein, H. (1996). *Multilevel statistical models*. London, UK: Edward Arnold.

Graubard, B., & Korn, E. (1996). Modeling the sampling design in the analysis of health surveys. *Statistical Methods in Medical Research*, 5(3), 263–281.

Green, J. L., Camilli, G., & Elmore, P. B. (2006). *Handbook of complementary methods in education research*. Mahwah, NJ: Lawrence Erlbaum Associates.

Grilli, L., & Pratesi, M. (2004). Weighted estimation in multilevel ordinal and binary models in the presence of informative sampling design. *Survey Methodology*, 30(1), 93–103.

Hox, J. J. (1995). *Applied multilevel analysis*. Amsterdam, the Netherlands: TT-Publikaties.

Hox, J. J. (1998). Multilevel modeling: When and why. In I. Balderjahn, R. Mathar, & M. Schader (Eds.), *Classification, data analysis, and data highways* (pp. 147–154). New York, NY: Springer.

Joncas, M. (2008). TIMSS 2007 sampling design. In J. F. Olson, M. O. Martin, & I. V. S. Mullis (Eds.), *TIMSS 2007 technical report* (pp. 76–93). Chestnut Hill, MA: Boston College.

Kish, L. (1965). *Survey sampling*, New York, NY: Wiley.

Knapp, T. R. (1977). The unit-of-analysis problem in applications of simple correlation analysis to educational research. *Journal of Educational Statistics*, 2(3), 171–186.

Koretz, D., McCaffrey, D., & Sullivan, T. (2001). Predicting variations in mathematics performance in four countries using TIMSS. *Education Policy Analysis Archives*, 9(34), 28 pp. Retrieved from http://epaa.asu.edu/epaa/v9n34/

Korn, E. L., & Graubard, B. I. (1995). Analysis of large health surveys: Accounting for the sampling design. *Journal of the Royal Statistical Society*, 158(Series A), 263–295.

Korn, E. L., & Graubard, B. I. (2003). Estimating variance components by using survey data. *Journal of the Royal Statistical Society*, 65(Series B), 175–190.

Kovacevic, M. S., & Rai, S. N. (2003). A pseudo maximum likelihood approach to multilevel modeling of survey data. *Communications in Statistics, Theory and Methods*, 32, 103–121.

Kreft, I. G. G. (1996). *Are multilevel techniques necessary? An overview, including simulation studies*. Unpublished manuscript, California State University, Los Angeles.

Lamb, S. & Fullarton, S. (2001). *Classroom and school factors affecting mathematics achievement: A comparative study of the US and Australia using TIMSS*. Camberwell, Victoria, Australia: Australian Council for Educational, Research (ACER). Available online at http://research.acer.edu.au/timss_monographs/10.

Lohr, S. L. (1999). *Sampling: Design and analysis*. Pacific Grove, CA: Duxbury Press.

Longford, N. T. (1993). *Random coefficient models*. Oxford, UK: Clarendon Press.

Longford, N. T. (1996). Model-based variance estimation in surveys with stratified clustered designs. *Australian Journal of Statistics*, 38, 333–352.

Lubienski, S. T., & Lubienski, C. (2006). School sector and academic achievement: A multi-level analysis of NAEP mathematics data. *American Educational Research Journal*, 43(4), 651–698.

Ma, X., & McIntyre, L. J. (2005). Exploring differential effects of mathematics courses on mathematics achievement. *Canadian Journal of Education*, *28*(4), 827–852.

Maas, C. J. M., & Hox, J. J. (2005). Sufficient sample sizes for multilevel modeling. *Methodology 2005*, *1*(3), 86–92.

Martin, M. O., Mullis, I. V. S., & Kennedy, A. M. (2007). *PIRLS 2006 technical report*. Chestnut Hill, MA: Boston College.

Masters, G. N., & Wright, B. D. (1997). The partial credit model. In W. J. Van der Linden, & R. K. Hambleton (Eds.), *Handbook of modern item response theory* (pp. 101–122). New York, NY: Springer.

Moerbeek, M., Van Breukelen, G. J. P., & Berger, M. P. F. (2000). Design issues for experiments in multilevel populations. *Journal of Educational and Behavioral Statistics*, *25*(3), 271–284.

Moerbeek, M., Van Breukelen, G. J. P., & Berger, M. P. F. (2001). Optimal experimental design for multilevel logistic models. *Journal of the Royal Statistical Society, Series D (The Statistician)*, *50*(1), 17–30.

Mok, M. (1995). Sample size requirements for 2-level designs in educational research. *Multilevel Modelling Newsletter*, *7*(2), 11–15.

Muthén, B. O. (2008, March 3). *Mplus discussion: Adjusting sampling errors for cluster sampling*. Retrieved from http://www.statmodel.com/discussion/messages/12/305.html

Muthén, L. K., & Muthén, B. O. (2002). How to use a Monte Carlo study to decide on sample size and determine power. *Structural Equation Modeling*, *9*(4), 599–620.

Muthén, L. K., & Muthén, B. O. (2008). *Mplus user's guide* (5th ed.). Los Angeles, CA: Muthén & Muthén.

Okumura, T. (2007). Sample size determination for hierarchical linear models considering uncertainty in parameter estimates. *Behaviormetrika*, *34*(2), 79–93.

Olson, J. F., Martin, M. O., & Mullis, I. V. S. (Eds.). (2008). *TIMSS 2007 technical report*. Chestnut Hill, MA: Boston College.

Organisation for Economic Co-operation and Development (OECD). (2006). *PISA 2006 technical report*. Paris, France: Author.

Organisation for Economic Co-operation and Development (OECD). (2009). *PISA data analysis manual: SAS, second edition. Education and skills*. Paris, France: Author.

Pfeffermann, D., Moura, F., & Silva, P. (2006). Multilevel modeling under informative sampling. *Biometrika*, *4*, 943–959.

Pfeffermann, D., Skinner, C. J., Holmes, D. J., Goldstein, H., & Rabash, J. (1998). Weighting for unequal selection probabilities in multilevel models. *Journal of the Royal Statistical Society, Series B. Statistical Methodology*, *60*, 23–56.

Pong, S., & Pallas, A. (2001). Class size and eighth-grade math achievement in the United States and abroad. *Educational Evaluation and Policy Analysis*, *23*(3), 251–273.

Rabe-Hesketh, S., & Skrondal, A. (2006). Multilevel modelling of complex survey data. *Journal of the Royal Statistical Society*, *169*(4), 805–827.

Rasch, G. (1980). *Probabilistic models for some intelligence and attainment tests* (expanded ed.). Chicago, IL: University of Chicago Press.

Raudenbush, S. W. (1988). Educational applications of hierarchical linear models: A review. *Journal of Educational Statistics*, *13*(2), 85–116.

Raudenbush, S. W. (1997). Statistical analysis and optimal design for cluster randomized trials. *Psychological Methods*, *2*, 173–185.

Raudenbush, S. W., & Bryk, A. S. (1986). A hierarchical model for studying school effects. *Sociology of Education*, *59*, 1–17.

Raudenbush, S. W., Spybrook, J., Liu, X., & Congdon, R. (2005). *Optimal design for longitudinal and multilevel research (Version 1.55)* [computer software]. Chicago, IL: University of Chicago Press.

Reise, S. P., & Duan, N. (2003). Design issues in multilevel studies. In S. P. Reise & N. Duan (Eds.), *Multilevel modeling: Methodological advances, issues, and applications* (pp. 285–298). Mahwah, NJ: Lawrence Erlbaum.

Robinson, W. S. (1950). Ecological correlations and the behavior of individuals. *American Sociological Review*, *15*, 351–357.

Rogosa, D. (1978). Politics, process, and pyramids. *Journal of Educational Statistics*, *3*(1), 79–86.

Rumberger, R. W. (1995). Dropping out of middle school: A multilevel analysis of students and schools. *American Educational Research Journal*, *32*, 583–625.

Rutkowski, L., Gonzalez, E., Joncas, M., & von Davier, M. (2010). International large-scale assessment data: Issues in secondary analysis and reporting. *Educational Researcher*, *39*(2), 142–151.

Sarndal, C.-E., Swenson, B., & Wretman, J. (1992). *Model assisted survey sampling*. New York, NY: Springer-Verlag.

Scherbaum, C. A., & Ferreter, J. M. (2009). Estimating statistical power and required sample sizes for organizational research using multilevel modeling. *Organizational Research Methods*, *12*(2), 347–367.

Schulz, W. (2006, April). *Measuring the socio-economic background of students and its effect on achievement in PISA 2000 and PISA 2003*. Paper presented at the annual meeting of the American Educational Research Association, San Francisco, CA.

Snijders, T. (2005). Power and sample size in multilevel linear models. In B. S. Everitt & D. C. Howell (Eds.), *Encyclopedia of statistics in behavioral science* (Vol. 3, pp. 1570–1573). Chichester, UK: Wiley.

Snijders, T. (2006). Sampling. In A. Leyland & H. Goldstein (Eds.), *Multilevel modelling of health statistic*s (pp. 159–174). New York, NY: Wiley.

Snijders, T., & Bosker, R. (1993). Standard errors and sample sizes for two-level research. *Journal of Educational Statistics*, *18*(3), 237–259.

Snijders, T., & Bosker, R. (1999). *An introduction to basic and advanced multilevel modeling*. Thousand Oaks, CA: Sage.

Stapleton, L. (2002). The incorporation of sample weights into multilevel structural equation models. *Structural Equation Modeling*, *9*(4), 475–502.

Suárez-Orozco, M. M., & Qin-Hilliard, D. (2004). *Globalization: Culture and education for a new millennium*. Berkeley, CA: University of California Press.

Thomas, L. T., & Heck, R. H. (2001). Analysis of large scale secondary data in higher education research: Potential perils associated with complex sampling designs. *Research in Higher Education*, *42*(5), 517–540.

Van der Leeden, R., Busing, F., & Meijer, E. (1997). *Applications of bootstrap methods for two-level models*. Paper presented at the Multilevel Conference, Amsterdam, the Netherlands.

Von Davier, M., Gonzalez, E., & Mislevy, R. J. (2009). What are plausible values and why are they useful? *IERI Monograph Series (2): Issues and methodologies in large-scale assessments* (pp. 9–36). Hamburg, Germany: IEA-ETS Research Institute.

Wang, J. (1998). Opportunity to learn: The impacts and policy implications. *Educational Evaluation and Policy Analysis*, *20*(3), 137–156.

Wenglinsky, H. (2002). How schools matter: The link between teacher classroom practices and student academic performance. *Education Policy Analysis Archives*, *10*(12). Retrieved from http://epaa.asu.edu/epaa/v10n12/

Willms, J. D. (2003). *Ten hypotheses about socioeconomic gradients and community differences in children's developmental outcomes*. Ottawa, Ontario, Canada: Applied Research Branch, Human Resources Development Canada.

Willms, J. D., & Shields, M. (1996). *A measure of socioeconomic status for the national longitudinal study of children*. Draft prepared as a reference for researchers conducting analysis of the first wave of data from the Canadian National Longitudinal Study of Children and Youth (NLSCY).

Wu, M. (2010). Measurement, sampling, and equating errors in large-scale assessments. *Educational Measurement: Issues and Practice*, *29*(4), 15–27.

Zaccarin, S., & Donati, C. (2008). *The effects of sampling weights in multilevel analysis of PISA data* (working paper no. 119). Trieste, Italy: University of Trieste. Retrieved from http://www2.units.it/nirdses/sito_inglese/working%20papers/files%20for%20wp/wp119.pdf

INFORMATION FOR CONTRIBUTORS

Content

IERI Monograph Series: Issues and Methodologies in Large-Scale Assessments is a joint publication between the International Association for the Evaluation of Educational Achievement (IEA) and Educational Testing Service (ETS). The goal of the publication is to contribute to the science of large-scale assessments so that the best available information is provided to policy-makers and researchers from around the world. Papers accepted for this publication are those that focus on improving the science of large-scale assessments and that make use of data collected by programs such as IEA-TIMSS, IEA-PIRLS, IEA-Civics, IEA-SITES, U.S.-NAEP, OECD-PISA, OECD-PIAAC, IALS, ALL, etc.

If you have questions or concerns about whether your paper adheres to the purpose of the series, please contact us at IERInstitute@iea-dpc.de.

Style

The style guide for all IERI publications is the *Publication Manual of the American Psychological Association* (5th ed., 2001). Manuscripts should be typed on US letter or A4 format, upper and lower case, double spaced in its entirety, with one-inch margins on all sides. The type size should be 12 point. Subheads should be at reasonable intervals to break the monotony of lengthy text. Pages should be numbered consecutively at the bottom of the page, beginning with the page after the title page. Mathematical symbols and Greek letters should be clearly marked to indicate italics, boldface, superscript, and subscript.

Author Identification

The complete title of the article and the name of the author(s) should be typed only on the submission form to ensure anonymity in the review process. The pages of the paper should have no author names, but may carry a short title at the top. Information in the text or references that would identify the author should be deleted from the manuscript (e.g., text citations of "my previous work," especially when accompanied by a self-citation; a preponderance of the author's own work in the reference list). These may be reinserted in the final draft. The author (whether first-named or co-author) who will be handling the correspondence with the editor and working with the publications people should submit complete contact information, including a full mailing address, telephone number, and email addresses.

Review Process

Papers will be acknowledged by the managing editor upon receipt. After a preliminary internal editorial review by IERI staff, articles will be sent to two external reviewers who have expertise in the subject of the manuscript. The review process takes approximately three to six months. You should expect to hear from the editor within that time regarding the status of your manuscript. IERI uses a blind review system, which means the identity of the authors is not revealed to the reviewers. In order to be published as part of the monograph series, the work will undergo and receive favorable technical, substantive, and editorial review.

Originality of Manuscript and Copyright

Manuscripts are accepted for consideration with the understanding that they are original material and are not under consideration for publication elsewhere. If another version of the paper is being considered by another publication, or has been or will be published elsewhere (even as a working paper), authors should clearly indicate this at the time.

To protect the works of authors and the institute, we copyright all of our publications. Rights and permissions regarding the uses of IERI-copyrighted materials are handled by the IERI executive board. Authors who wish to use material, such as figures or tables, for which they do not own the copyright must obtain written permission from IERInstitute and submit it to IERI with their manuscripts.

Comments and Grievances

The Publications Committee welcomes comments and suggestions from authors. Please send these to the committee at IERInstitute@iea-dpc.de.

The right-of-reply policy encourages comments on articles recently published in an IERI publication. Such comments are subject to editorial review and decision. If the comment is accepted for publication, the editor will inform the author of the original article. If the author submits a reply to the comment, the reply is also subject to editorial review and decision.

If you think that your manuscript is not reviewed in a careful or timely manner and in accordance with standard practices, please call the matter to the attention of the institute's executive board.

Publication Schedule

The IERI Monograph is published annually, in October. Manuscripts can be submitted for review any time of the year. Most fitting to the review and editing process would be to submit a paper around 12 months before the monograph's publication date.

Manuscripts are reviewed and processed in the order they are received, and are published in the next available monograph if accepted for publication. If manuscripts move through the review and editing process considerably before publication of the print version, IERI offers an online version of it on the IERI website, in advance of its publication in the upcoming volume.

Each monograph consists of five to seven research papers. If, in a single year, there are more than seven accepted manuscripts, the editorial committee will determine whether the manuscript(s) will be published in the following monograph or in an additional monograph in the same year.

Submission of Articles

The monograph series *IERI Issues and Methodologies in Large-scale Assessment* welcomes the submission of original, research-based articles, in English. Manuscripts should be between 7,000 and 10,000 words in length, including abstract, notes, and references.

All contributors must submit:

- The text of the paper in editable format;
- All included tables and figures in editable format;
- A 100- to 150-word abstract briefly describing the content and central hypothesis of the paper;
- A completed article submission form, which can be found below or obtained from the IERI website: www.ierinstitute.org

IERI accepts only electronic submissions. Please send the manuscript to be considered for publication and any supplemental files (graphs and tables) to ierinstitute@iea-dpc.de.